# About The Cover

I0140558

The cover is from a sketch by Dave Risk (1865-1933). Risk, of Weston, Missouri, was one of the most accomplished livestock artists of his time. He was often commissioned to draw grand champions at stock shows, doing so for both individual owners and nationally circulated magazines.

The original of this Hopley print (bearing a date that is blurred but appears to be 1910) hangs in an office in the Chicago area, owned by a grandson of Wayland and Helen Hopley. The copper printing plate is in the possession of another grandson; one living in Hawaii.

Reproductions were made and the scene appears on Hopley sale bills and other promotional material from the early 1900s.

The print used for this book cover was owned by Minnie Hopley Muffley, a daughter of Peter and Edna. In the lower right corner is an automobile with a youthful driver and a slender lady in a white gown. Her face may be veiled. Below the car Minnie has written words that are only partially decipherable. Some think they say "Wayland & Mamma." Others read it as "Wayland at ?????" with the lower word in question.

The house appears to be that of Harry and Della on the West Side Place. The barns, though, are painted with words "Riverside Farms," and "Peter Hopley's Imported Horses." Those barns were on Peter's place east of the river.

The original does not include the automobile. Who added it, when and why, we don't know. In 1910 Wayland would have been sixteen, his mother was approaching fifty. Minnie and Fred Muffley were married in 1911. Readers may draw their own conclusions as to when and why the automobile was added, and who is depicted in the scene. I doubt that Risk drew the car, as it's out of proportion—too small in comparison to the horses and man near it—and this would not have been characteristic of Risk.

There are other questions raised by the drawing that probably cannot, at this late date, be answered.

# HOPLEY

*by*

## ROY MARSHALL

*with*

## JANEILLE KENWORTHY

aventine press

Copyright © 2015, Roy Marshall
First Edition

Without limiting the rights under copyright reserved above,
no part of this publication may be reproduced, stored in or introduced into
a retrieval system, or transmitted, in any form or by any means (electronic,
mechanical, photocopying, recording, or otherwise),
without the prior written permission of both the copyright owner
and the publisher of this book.

Published by Aventine Press
55 East Emerson St.
Chula Vista CA 91911
www.aventinepress.com

ISBN: 978-1-59330- 876--6

Printed in the United States of America
ALL RIGHTS RESERVED

# Acknowledgements

My sincere thanks to Janeille Kenworthy, who did much of the research into the genealogy of the Hopley family. Her name is on the cover, and deservedly so. The book was difficult, in part, because the Hopleys re-used names to an extent that make it confusing to know which Margaret, which Thomas, which Edna and Peter was being referred to. There were also nicknames applied to different Hopleys of different generations. We tried to clarify this by referring to old Pete as Peter, his grandson as Pete; Wayland, Jr. as "Hickory," and so on.

We made every effort to avoid errors in the names, but newspapers and other documents often mistakenly referred a Hopley by an incorrect name, and I may have as well.

Contributions of family members are much appreciated. The late Minnie Hopley Muffley retained a treasure of photographs and newspaper clippings. They are now in the possession of a grandson, Richard Muffley, who was extremely helpful.

We spoke with numerous other descendants of Peter and Edna Hopley. Some were cooperative and, understandably, some were not.

Libraries cannot receive enough credit for what they do.

For earlier books and magazine articles I relied on local libraries, including those in Griswold and Anita. For this one Ms. Kenworthy spent hours in the Atlantic library. I was often there as well, and also in Lewis.

The cooperation of the entire staff in these places, their understanding and helpfulness, was all that could have been hoped for and more.

Susie Campbell, the long-time librarian in Lewis and a friend since our school days, is retiring as I'm finishing this book. She didn't want a retirement coffee, so I doubt she'd appreciate any special recognition here.

Regardless, after dedicating an earlier book to my wife, a later one to my mother, this one is for Susie and all the libraries and librarians of Cass County.

# Forward

I began researching the Hopley family when I was about thirteen. This was a difficult age for a boy at Halloween; too old to extort candy door-to-door, too young to join marauding gangs in their outhouse tipping adventures.

That year I went to an apple-bobbing, donkey-tail-pinning party in the church basement. As an unexciting evening was wearing down a classmate (I think it was Harry) suggested we go to a haunted house. He knew where there was one and how to get in. Five or six of us set out, including a couple of girls.

I'd ridden my bicycle past the Hopley mansion on a daily newspaper route, but never paid it much attention. Vacant, sagging, in need of paint, the lawn grown to weeds, the house was anything but welcoming. It was made less so by a wrought iron fence and gate with a chain and lock.

We followed Harry through someone's back yard to a place where the rail fence had fallen or been pushed. Entering a porch, we passed through a small and unimpressive kitchen. The rest of the house, though, was like something from a Vincent Price movie. The eerie beams of three or four flashlights revealed high ceilings, glass chandeliers, built-in hardwood cupboards and book cases, all covered with dust and cobwebs. Had there been someone who knew the story and related how twenty-year-old Beulah Hopley, home on a break from college and helping her mother serve breakfast, suffered a violent and fatal seizure in the dining room we were standing in, I'm sure the girls would have

1

shrieked in terror.

Without doubt they would have shuddered had we known the body of old Peter Hopley reposed in a coffin in the large central room (called the parlor) prior to his funeral in 1926.

That room, with a glass-enclosed alcove, had also been the site of gala parties, of sumptuous feasts served to scores of guests—distinguished guests who dined on fresh and exotic seafood, fattened geese, choice Hopley beef, fruit and nuts from Peter's California farms, all prepared and presented by hired staff.

Down the stairs to that parlor, pausing at each step, had marched Hopley daughters. Veiled and gowned and waiting at the final step until the pianist changed pages and hit the first rousing chord of Mendelssohn's Wedding March, clutching Peter's strong right arm as they passed through an aisle in a sea of guests.

I followed Harry up the wide stairway, gripping a walnut bannister, and along a hall opening onto several bedrooms. I remember red carpet; red shag carpet that, even to a youth with no sense of fashion, was garish and out of place.

We passed a large mirror, saw our reflections, and I wanted out. I didn't feel fright, rather a vague sense that I was as foreign in that place as cheap carpet. The girls had enough as well. Harry laughed.

Some went back the next year. The house became a destination of Halloween partiers, then a target for vandals and thieves. I've been told it was defaced, stripped of valuables, stained glass was broken and bats moved in. I went by one day when it was being torn down, work done by friends of mine, and I was curious and thought about going inside.

Now, having learned what I have of the Hopley family of Lewis, I would relish few things more than the chance to browse through their mansion. I've paid my dues, taken the journey. I know Peter and Edna as well as I ever will. I think they'd invite me in, let me learn more of their lives and times. But then I knew nothing of them, didn't belong in their home any more than did the awful shag that Mrs. Croghan put down. So I stayed out.

Only now, after resuming my research a few decades following that Halloween night, have I ventured to go back.

# Chapter One

*Nancy Hopley, 16, of Atlantic died at 10:15 Saturday at Immanuel Hospital in Omaha, where she had been a patient for two weeks. Miss Hopley had been ill and was hospitalized here prior to being taken to the Omaha hospital. (Atlantic News Telegraph, July 11, 1966)*

On a warm midsummer afternoon a hearse, bearing discrete markings that identified the Roland Funeral Home, turned off the old White Pole Road and passed slowly under a weathered metal sign. On both sides of the narrow driveway were tombstones, some more than a century old, nearly all of them permanently shaded by a grove of towering cedars. The Oakwood Cemetery near Lewis had, for whatever reason, grown more to cedar and pine than oak.

While gravestones all represent a story, most of those the hearse passed by had largely been forgotten. West of the original Hopley plot, cracked and leaning slightly to the east, was a slender marble tablet, once white but now a bleak gray, bearing the faded name of Mary Coffin. Mary had not fared well, and neither had her marker. Next to hers, in better shape although only a few weeks newer, was that of her husband, Eli. Mrs. Coffin, during the exceptionally cold winter of 1872-73, died under suspicious circumstances. There were indications that she had been abused, starved, neglected—perhaps even poisoned— by her husband. Evidence was gathered during a brief investigation, after which a grand jury indicted Eli Coffin. The charge was murder.

On a Saturday night in early February, with the trial due to convene on Monday, Coffin was accosted by group of unidentified men. He was struck on the head with a blunt object, shot, then hung by the neck from Turkey Creek Bridge. The following day his frozen corpse was cut down, thawed, an autopsy performed, after which he was buried beside his wife. Prevailing public opinion held that Coffin, who most agreed got what was coming to him, was done in by a group led by Mary's brother. Names were named. Women huddled together and whispered. Men sat around wood burners in town stores and talked. They didn't, however, have much to tell authorities. The investigation into Coffin's death seems to have lacked enthusiasm and concluded without an arrest.

Peter Hopley returned from the west only months before Coffin was lynched. While he played no part in the case, he must have known at least some of those involved. As a boy, Peter's father farmed near the Coffin cabin. For several years Coffin operated a dry goods store only a couple of blocks from where Peter's parents lived when they moved to Lewis. Peter's first farm was an eighty-acre place not far from where Mary Coffin's emaciated body was found.

A passer-by unaware of the story might read the inscription, the dates, and assume wedded bliss—that Mr. Coffin, grieving for his dearly departed, had lingered for a month, then succumbed of a broken heart.

Hopley and his family associated, and had business dealings with, Oliver Mills. The Mills monument, only a few steps removed from that of Mary and Eli Coffin, stands in sharp contrast. Mills, an early and distinguished resident of Lewis, was active in many causes. A staunch Republican, he assisted in the operation of the Underground Railroad that passed through the area. Remaining politically active after the Civil War, Mills held numerous local and state offices, including a stint as president of the State Board of Agriculture. He speculated in land, bought and sold cattle and horses and, if he didn't become wealthy, he was comfortable. Folklore has it that as old age settled in and Mills reflected on his past and contemplated the future, he reached the conclusion that he was deserving of the most impressive edifice in Oakwood Cemetery. While his is a fine, massive monument, others show more imagination.

Old Peter Hopley might have put up a bigger one—he could certainly afford it and his achievements were many—but such was not the case. The centerpiece on the Peter Hopley family plot, near that of his parents, is large but plain. No pillars, lambs, angels, scrollwork or ostentatious engravings. He let Mills have a bigger one and others have the frills. The stone chosen was a slab of polished granite five foot wide, five foot tall and twenty inches thick. It bears but a single word: Hopley.

Among the stones that few, if any, were likely to notice as the procession passed by was an inexpensive, knee-high and moss-covered sliver of rock bearing the nearly unreadable inscription: "Gertrude Hopley Wife of John Hopley," below which was the year of her death. The choice of words is perhaps misleading, as at the time of her passing she was most definitely not the wife of Peter Hopley's older brother, John. She had, according to news articles, a "most unhappy marriage." Two years before she died, the Telegraph related, she had ingested a toxic substance. Whether this contributed to her end is unknown, but she would never regain her health. She did, however, recover enough to file for divorce. Shortly after becoming the former Mrs. John Hopley, she died. John arranged for the funeral, which was held in his home.

The hearse stopped near an open grave. Cars filed past as pall bearers, mostly classmates of the deceased, assembled. Vehicles were still coming from the north as the casket was carried under a Roland's canopy and, with an appropriate wreath on top, put in place. A Methodist minister named Robert McBlain, bible in hand, waited while the family assembled, while more cars parked and the crowd continued to form.

A girl who has lived just 16 years, 2 months and 12 days, especially a popular girl from a prominent family; a girl who had just finished her sophomore year in high school and was looking forward to being a junior, a girl who died after a relatively brief illness, is likely to have a big funeral.

Nancy Hopley had a name with an allure, an association with a dynasty. Her ancestors were local legends, well-known and respected even far from the crop and livestock empire they founded in Cass County. And if her parents fought, if her father was an abuser and a womanizer, her uncle obnoxious when drunk—which he often was—if the Hopley fortune was wasting away, it wasn't Nancy's fault. Circumstances, in fact, probably made her even more interesting.

At the fringe of the crowd was Mrs. Louise Hunt. Louise was not well-acquainted with Nancy or her siblings, but she knew the parents and grandparents and lived on a farm near theirs for much of her life. She recalls that, shortly after the graveside service finally got under way, a friend tugged her sleeve and pointed, rather excitedly, toward a man.

"Froggy" Goeken was a hard-drinking carouser, the son of a well-to-do farmer and high school agriculture teacher. He knew and had been a neighbor to Wayland Hopley, Jr., the son of an even more well-to-do farmer. Wayland was called, by Goeken and most everyone who knew him, either "Junior" or "Hickory." Hickory was, at that moment, near the casket with his estranged wife, three surviving daughters, and a son, Wayland III. Also with him were his parents, his brother, Pete, and other family members.

Mrs. Hunt did not, at first glance, notice anything unusual about Goeken. That he was at the funeral was not a surprise. He was without a jacket, but so were other men on that July day. Then she saw it. On Goeken's belt was a holster. He had not only brought a revolver to the service, he was wearing it for all to see.

As the minister offered words of comfort another car entered the cemetery. It was unmarked, and the man who emerged was not wearing a uniform. He was, however, well known by most in attendance.

Bob Voggesser was a burly, barrel-bellied man who, when not in the public view, could be as loud and profane as Hickory Hopley. "Voggie," though, had a different calling. He was then Cass County's deputy sheriff. He would later run for sheriff and, he recalls with a degree of pride, carry every precinct.

On that day in 1966 he circled the assemblage, spotted the man he sought, walked directly to him. He placed his hand on Hickory Hopley's arm. "Come with me," Voggesser said, "you're under arrest."

Many of those in the crowd were unaware of what was taking place. Helen Haw Hopley, close enough to Voggesser she could have slapped him, watched her oldest living son be led away. She was seething, vowed there'd be hell to pay.

# Chapter Two

One hundred years before Nancy Hopley's death, Samuel Reed was working in a place he wasn't sure he'd get out of alive. Reed was a surveyor and construction supervisor during the building of the Trans-continental Railroad (1863-1869). On May 27, 1867, with the Union Pacific tracks pushing from North Platte toward Cheyenne, he wrote his wife that Indians had raided a nearby ranch and ran off a considerable amount of livestock. Five days later he wrote that Indians had killed four laborers. "When men go to work," he continued, "even in full sight of camp, they go heavily armed."

War parties of Sioux and Cheyenne were never far away. Raid followed raid; some merely harassing, others deadly. A group of four whites carrying mail were ambushed, mutilated and scalped near Laramie. Surveyors watched from a distance as miles of survey stakes, markers they'd worked for days to precisely place, were pulled and used for Indian campfires. Livestock was stolen, fires were set. Two more surveyors were killed in June. In August a train was derailed. There were only a few passengers, nearly all of which were killed. Two of those spared were white women, taken alive for amusement.

Army officers in charge of protection included Civil War veterans such as General William Tecumseh Sherman. Sherman knew a major step in eliminating what was called "the Indian problem" was to complete the railroad. Buffalo, it was said, would not cross the tracks. Horses did so with reluctance. Dividing tribal territory weakened them, while the ability to move men and supplies by rail was a white advantage that could not be overcome. Indian leaders, many of them, understood and did their fighting for a strategic purpose. Others harassed whites for the scalps, the loot, the glory and the sheer hell of it.

Generally speaking, the nearer the main railroad camps the safer a person was. Those who ventured away were in the greatest danger.

Peter Hopley (1847-1926) hauled supplies to remote areas between camps and, when he sat down at the age of seventy to write a brief memoir he called "How I Became a Millionaire," he was probably telling it like it was when he noted that *"fights with Indians were almost a daily occurrence."* If war parties weren't enough, most of the camps had their own hazards. Cheap whiskey, gambling, loose women, card sharks and thieves were part of a camp-following assemblage that came to be called "Hell on Wheels." When a card player complained about cheating, or a customer protested a pocket-picking prostitute, that person was more likely to be shot than pacified.

Railroad camps and Indian Territory between them were not a place for the timid. Peter Hopley not only survived, he prospered.

Adventure was not a new experience for Hopley. Records show he was seven years old when his parents and several siblings left England to settle in America. Peter probably was not with them, although accounts differ. His father was said to be following the lead of a brother who had migrated to this country a few years earlier (this was probably not a brother, but one or more of his older sons).

The various versions, all offered as factual accounts, of how the family of Thomas and Francis Arrowsmith Hopley came to this country, have curious differences. One has to do with when and how Peter and Hannah made the journey.

We know with certainty that in 1854 the children consisted of Margaret, age 23, John, 22, Thomas, 21, (John and Thomas came to America in June of 1849. They sailed on the *Water Witch* into the port of New Orleans, then by steamboat up the Mississippi to Burlington, settling in or near the town of Denmark. Thomas died there prior to 1856). Other children were William, 18 (he arrived in New York on the ship *Roscius* on September 20, 1853), Anne, 15, James, 13, Hannah, 11, Francis, 9, Peter, 7, and Joseph, 4. Tickets were purchased for some of the family still in England, but it seems not for all. (An eleventh child, Edwin, was born in 1852 and died eight months later.)

The *Black Hawk* was built in 1853. Her maiden voyage began on April 4, 1854, when she sailed out of Liverpool, England, bound for New York. The Hopley family—most of them—were on this ship. Records of "wrecksite-eu," an online data base of information on ships lost at sea, show that on April 17 the *Black Hawk* was beset by a hurricane. De-masted and helpless in the water, she floundered at sea for a week. Passengers were eventually picked up by several other ships that chanced upon the *Black Hawk*. These included the *Caroline*, the *Dirigio* (which in turn transferred some passengers to the *Elizabeth Duncan)*, and the *Currituck*. The last crew members left on April 24, leaving the *Black Hawk* to sink at her leisure.

Now come the details.

According to a biographical sketch published during his lifetime, William Hopley, born in England in 1836, ran away from home at the age of seventeen. He and an older brother, John, who had come here previously then returned to England, made another journey to this country, arriving in New York. William found work as a machinist in Jersey City. He and John wrote good things about America and their parents decided to relocate.

A history of Cass County largely agrees, telling us the family sailed on the *Black Hawk*, a new ship of the well-known White Star Line, in April of 1854. Three weeks out a fierce storm was encountered, a storm that, after two days of pounding, snapped the mast and swept away most of the superstructure. When the storm subsided the liner was still afloat, but taking on water and without sails. The deck was swamped. Children were said to be standing on tables, men and women knee deep, the able-bodied bailing water, none having anything to eat but hardtack for several days.

Minnie Hopley Muffley, a daughter of Peter, would listen years later as her father and other relatives described the incident. As she remembered it being told to her (and related by her grandson, Richard Muffley), Peter and Francis had brought onboard a quantity of valuable personal belongings that included guns, bolts of cloth, an inherited silver dinner set and other pieces. The storm subsided on the third day. Flares attracted other ships and the Hopleys were taken aboard the *Elizabeth Duncan* (they probably were taken first on the *Dirigio,* then transferred.) As lifeboats were lowered the directive was "women and children first." Francis sent the children, Margaret tending to Peter and Hannah, but she herself refused to go without her husband, who was quite ill. When they did leave the floundering *Black Hawk* they could take only what they were wearing. Thomas had on a money belt containing about $500, but everything else was lost. While the family was reunited, to the immense relief and pleasure of all, there was also bad news—the *Elizabeth Duncan* was on her way back to England. The family spent several days in a Poorhouse near Falmouth before embarking a second time. This trip went without incident, but upon landing at Ellis Island it was learned that two of the younger children, Peter and Hannah, had scarlet fever. They were not allowed to leave the ship. Margaret, the oldest, was placed in charge of her ill siblings and returned with them to England. A brother, William, stayed in the New York area. He got a job, saved his money until he had enough for their passage, then sent for Margaret, Hannah, and Peter. (The family liked to re-use names, which can lead to confusion. Peter's name went to several descendants. He would name his second daughter Margaret, doing so for a sister he greatly admired.)

A somewhat different version was carried in the Atlantic News Telegraph Farm Monthly in June of 1947. The piece appears under the headline "Shipwreck and Gold Rush in Background of Hopley Ranch." Written by Marilyn Simpson, a daughter of then publisher Fred Simpson, she seems to have relied primarily on an interview with Peter's youngest son, Wayland Hopley. This account has Francis Elizabeth Arrowsmith being born into nobility. The daughter of Lord Arrowsmith, she married a commoner and incurred the wrath of her parents. Thomas Hopley, a Cheshire merchant (some accounts say he was a pharmacist), and his bride were essentially disowned, banished from the Arrowsmith family.

Wayland's account has it that after years of hard work and diligent saving they set out for America. They could not take all their children and decided the two youngest—Hannah (often referred to as Anna in newspaper articles, and perhaps called that by her family) and Peter would remain. Parents arranged for the children's care and departed.

Ms. Simpson's article says the ship capsized in the storm, *"and the passengers were left floating on the ocean. Somehow the Hopleys managed to climb onto a makeshift raft and, after floating around for several days with faint hope of rescue, they were picked up by another boat."* As for personal belongings, this account tells of Francis Hopley *"converting all these worldly possessions into cash before they left England, and she had placed all the cash in a money belt about her waist. The money belt had never been removed from its place of security, and her foresight was the factor that enabled them to turn around and head, once again, for America."*

This version has Peter and Hannah staying in England when the Black Hawk departed. Other family members arrived in New York, then traveled on to Lee County in Iowa. An exception was William. He remained on the east coast, found work, and saved until he had the funds to cover passage for his two younger siblings. The Simpson article has the family reuniting in Lee County (the year was 1856), then moving to the Lewis area. Eleven years later Peter went west in search of gold. Simpson's article tells us *"he had the luck. He came back with a stake and, to show his appreciation to brother Bill for all he had done, used the money to set them both up in cattle ranching."*

These accounts are interesting, although full of discrepancies. Immigration records have Margaret coming to America with her parents. It appears she neither remained in England nor returned there to take care of Peter and Hannah (which were not the youngest, as some articles state).

There's no doubt that Hannah and Peter were delayed two years in crossing. One account has them staying because Thomas and Francis "realized they couldn't take all their children." Wayland Hopley is quoted in the Simpson article as speculating the decision regarding who would remain behind was made by lottery, by drawing straws, or even, as he called it, by playing an English version of "odd man out."

We have to ask why Peter and Hannah couldn't go? On one hand it is implied the parents simply couldn't afford it, that William had to labor and save in order to raise money for the fare. And yet every source we've found remains consistent with regard to $500 being in a money belt worn by one of the parents. (The Simpson account has the belt

11

worn by Francis, others say it was Thomas, but this is a trivial point.) $500 was a sizeable sum and, with the average price of a ticket being between $8 and $20, money should not have been an issue. In addition to the $500 cash, belongings taken on board indicate the family was far from destitute, and could well have afforded passage for two more.

Several variations, some appearing in biographical sketches, others in obituaries and news articles, as well as that related later by Minnie Hopley Muffley, have Peter and Hannah on the Black Hawk, being taken by older sister Margaret in a life boat to the rescue ship, then making the return trip to England, back to the U.S., only to be turned back at Ellis Island, and so on.

Wayland, Minnie's younger brother, said Peter and Hannah were not on the Black Hawk. The ship's 1854 passenger list and 1856 census agree; those two were not part of the 1854 crossing.

So how did the scarlet fever story come to be? A possible explanation is that the two children came down with the disease just prior to departure. Believing them to be too sick to travel, or fearing they'd be turned back at Ellis Island, the parents left them temporarily behind. In the retelling of the shipwreck adventure Peter and Hannah were mistakenly included. That their parents "feared they'd be turned back because of the disease" became "they were turned back because of the disease." This, however, is only speculation—and does not explain why William waited two years.

Immigration records confirm that William went back to England in 1856. Bringing younger siblings, Hannah and Peter, they sailed for this country on the *Dreadnaught,* a three-mast sailing vessel that typically made the crossing in four to eight weeks. (One account has William saving the money for passage, then giving it to a ship's captain. The captain, so this story goes, was an honest man and on his next trip brought Peter and Hannah. Some details are all but impossible to sort out. This one was not. The names of all three siblings appear on the passenger list of the *Dreadnaught.*)

On some points the Simpson article is simply incorrect. One could take issue with the implication that Peter returned from the west with gold, a "stake" that allowed him to set William up in "cattle ranching."

This was not the case. William had a farm before Peter even went west. He farmed with his father in the late 1850s, started his own operation later, and was well established when Peter returned in 1872.

Many years later Peter wrote of the futility of seeking gold. He says that after returning from the west he and William went into a short-term partnership on some cattle. This could hardly be called setting his brother up in ranching. Simpson's article has the Hopley family floating for days on a makeshift raft. Every other account we're aware of has them remaining with other passengers on the disabled ship until rescued.

Marilyn Simpson was probably relating the story just as Wayland Hopley told it to her. Those who wrote various county histories and biographies were telling it, perhaps with a few embellishments, as it was related to them. There were, however, certain members of the Hopley family—including Wayland—of which some will say, even today, that they (as is the case with many) were more focused on a good story than factual details.

While the rather tedious and perhaps confusing maze of inconsistencies regarding how the Hopley family came to Cass County is not of particular importance, we relate them as an example. Peter, his brothers and sons, as well as his wife, were viewed in different ways by the people they knew. Some saw them as outstanding citizens, others thought the Hopleys—at least some of them—were scoundrels. Because Hopley men, and women, rose to a lofty position in Cass County business and social life, were well-traveled and widely known in the U.S. and abroad, they were closely covered by local newspapers. What the papers would print about them was not necessarily the way Hopley acquaintances and neighbors felt and not, in fact, always the way it was.

# Chapter Three

Shortly after William, Peter and Hannah joined their parents in Lee County, Thomas, Francis and other children still residing with them moved to Cass County, arriving during troublesome times. Lewis was barely a town, the slavery issue was dividing a nation, and Thomas had strong beliefs. He was an abolitionist. Lee County, while Thomas and his family lived there, was a hotbed of anti-slavery activity. Oliver Mills and Sophia Mills, along with James and Euphemia Baxter, were also in Lee County prior to relocating to Cass County, a move they made, at least in part, to work with Reverend Hitchcock and his Underground Railroad stopover. Thomas Hopley may have met Mills and Baxter in Lee County, may have been drawn to the Lewis area for some of the same reason. Like many who walked this path, the details of anti-slavery activities were shrouded, and much of what we have is folklore. (The Thomas Hopley obituary of 1871 does not mention his work with the Underground Railroad. It was only after his death that this phase of his life was made public.)

Older Hopley children scattered as they came of age, although some remained in Cass County. Hannah married Henry Wormington, who was a butcher in Lewis at the time. He wasn't a butcher for long, and neither did the young couple remain in Lewis.

Henry Wormington was born in England in 1832. At the age of 18 he entered into training as a meat cutter, serving six years as an apprentice and journeyman, most of it in London. In 1855 he came to

America, worked briefly at the Fulton meat market in New York, then moved on to Iowa. Two years later (1857) he married Hannah Hopley. Henry went into the wholesale meat business and did quite well. He might have remained in Lewis were it not for his health. He and Hannah moved to Colorado in 1863.

The trip west was probably as memorable as had been crossing the Atlantic. An article published years later in a Denver newspaper and reprinted in the Atlantic News Telegraph tells us that Hannah's first two children were born in Lewis, the three youngest in Colorado.

*They started across the plains in a wagon train bound for Denver. They arrived on the ill-fated night of April 18, the same night the Elephant Corral—headquarters for wagon trains stopping off for Denver—was burned. While her husband was away on an errand the fire broke out. Hannah Wormington devilishly harnessed one team of horses and hitched them to a wagon, while a hired man hitched the other to a second prairie schooner. With flames licking at the wagon bed beneath her feet, she started the horses. Frightened by the inferno, they balked. The young wife lashed out with a blacksnake whip, the horses bolted, and she and the two small children, who were huddled in the back of the wagon, were hurtled to safety. The wagon she had piloted, and that driven by the hired man, were the only two wagons saved. The rest were reduced to ashes in the blackened waste of the corral.*

Just how the "Elephant Corral" got the name is unknown. There was a similar haven for wagon trains in Council Bluffs also called the "Elephant Corral." One possibility for the name is depicted on a historical marker at the site in Denver. The beginning, the fire, and the demise of the place is described. In the gold rush days, the plaque tells us, and during other perilous crossings of the content, the term "seeing an elephant," became a metaphor for seeing something strange.

Hannah had other adventures:

*Riding alone near Littleton, she was surrounded by a band of Indians in a bad humor. Her pluck was rewarded by grunts of admiration from the braves, and she was finally allowed to go on, unharmed.*

According to the "History of Denver, Arapahoe County and Colorado," by O.L. Baskin & Co., published in 1880, the Wormingtons arrived in Denver and continued the line of work began in Lewis, except on a larger scale. Henry and Hannah bought a ten acre tract in Denver and built a slaughterhouse. He bought two lots at the corner of 17th and Champa Streets for $200. By the turn of the century the lots were valued at $100,000. When Hannah died in 1926 she still owned the Champa Street property, which was then reportedly bringing her an annual income of $250,000.

In the mid-1860s the Wormingtons purchased the 80 acre tract upon which Fort Logan was later established. When Baskin's history was published, Henry Wormington was a wealthy man. He and the former Hannah Hopley of Lewis had five children, the oldest son then a partner in the business. They owned several ranches and contracted with others for beef. Wormington & Co. was also in the wholesale vegetable trade, owning or leasing or contracting with producers in the Denver area.

Specifics of the illness that that took the family to Colorado were not mentioned in Baskin's history, but in 1871 Henry had problems with his eyes that threatened to leave him blind. He returned to England for treatment and, after a year, was cured.

The potential of the vegetable trade took him to California, where he began buying land in 1878. He would move to Lakeside, California, where he owned what his obituary referred to as a *large tract of land where he raised oranges and olives. He also owned property in the principal residential section of San Diego."* The Wormingtons did very well.

Young William Hopley married Mary Okell and bought farmland in Grove Township. Margaret married a Lewis carpenter and jack-of-all-trades named Otis Hardenberg and, a few years later, moved to Colorado. They didn't stay, however, returning to the Lewis area in 1892 and, shortly thereafter, were divorced. They had two children, Jesse and George. One of George's children was Frank Hardenberg, who farmed in Pottawattamie County before moving to Lewis. Another was George P. Hardenberg, born in 1909. George's mother, Hylinda Hondel Hardenberg, died shortly after George P. was born. His aunt Jesse, who had married into the Conn family, took him to raise (George Hardenberg took the name, and would be known as George Conn).

Anne, who arrived in this country at the age of 15, married Kellit T. Murdock. Murdock, originally from Indiana, lived in Lee County during the mid-1850s, came to Cass County in about 1856, and served in the Civil War. One of their daughters, Fanny, married Emery Woodward. Frances, two years older than Peter, married Ralph Okell.

The connections between the Hopley family and others having a multi-generational relationship with the Lewis area go on and on. When the Ladies Oakwood Cemetery Association was formed in 1892, the first president was Edna Everly Hopley, Peter's wife. This was appropriate, as she must have been related in one way or another to half the people buried on the original east side.

As older brothers left home—Thomas to Colorado, James to Kansas, John to the west and back—a bigger share of farm work fell to Peter. He was, by English custom, apprenticed to his father until the age of twenty-one.

Farm duties took precedence over school. As a teen-ager, Peter wrote, he attended country school for a part of one winter. He did not go back until years later. He was twenty, his father sixty-four, when Thomas sold the farm and moved to Lewis. Relieved of farm work, Thomas felt it was time for Peter to resume his formal education. The school he attended was located on the same lot as the present elementary building. Things did not go well. Peter was by far the oldest in his class. Being born and spending the first few years of his life in Cheshire, England, he retained a strong accent. Boys half his age teased and ridiculed him. After the first day of school he gave two or three of them a thrashing—easily done as Peter was a strapping six-footer; a man among boys. The beating didn't help. Tormenting resumed the following day. Peter later wrote that he decided to get his revenge by doing better than they, by becoming more successful than any of them.

When noon came and other students delved into their lunch boxes, Peter went home. He asked his father to release him from his apprenticeship obligation. Thomas told him to go back to school. Peter persisted. "Give me my time," he pleaded, "and let me go my own way." Thomas relented. Before the day ended Peter Hopley, with a team of oxen Thomas gave or loaned him, was headed west.

A few winter months as a teen-ager, a day and a half as a twenty-year-old, and Hopley's classroom experience was over. (This is according to him. We have to wonder why, with older brothers to help his father, he didn't go to school while living in England.)

His real education, he later commented, was about to begin.

He fell in initially with a group going to Pike's Peak hoping for gold. Near North Platte, Nebraska, the party paused in their journey to help bury several ranchers that had been killed by Indians. The experience might have caused Hopley to think the venture wasn't such a good idea. If so, he made no mention of it. He also fails to mention Hannah. As children they'd been through numerous ordeals, were close, and she'd gone to Colorado four years earlier. Although he surely visited Hannah and Henry, and they undoubtedly had Indian-related tales to tell, Peter's writing about that phase of his life focused on how he made money, not about family or social life.

The gold rush at Pike's Peak started a decade earlier and, by 1867, had largely fizzled out. Small amounts of gold were still being found, however, and fortune-seekers believed that if treasure was growing scarce at Pike's Peak, there were similar mountains all over Colorado.

In later years Peter expressed a dim view of the gold rush bunch. *"Men were driving daily over the richest soil the sun ever shone on, to seek a rocky soil where they hoped, often against hope, to strike it rich in gold."* He saw, perhaps mostly in retrospect, the fertile soil and lush grasslands of Iowa, Kansas, and Nebraska as being the real gold mine, one that would make a fortune for a man willing to work. In 1867, however, Peter Hopley left those fertile fields behind to join the chase for gold.

Reality soon set in. Others kept picking, digging, and panning. Peter Hopley, although he likely continued to seek gold from time to time, moved on.

Newspapers were full of coverage of the transcontinental railroad. Prospectors talked about it around the campfire. Miners and railroad workers mingled, some leaving one occupation to try the other.

What was taking place was one of the most remarkable engineering and construction feats in American history. Not until the Panama Canal was anything done to rival it. The project was too big for any one company, or even a conglomeration of railroads—even in the unlikely event they'd stop competing and work together. It had taken decades to make rail travel from the east coast to eastern Iowa possible. California and the west coast beckoned, but getting there took months of difficult and risky travel—whether by land or sea.

Abraham Lincoln is remembered for many things. Often overlooked is his role in the transcontinental railroad. Even before elected, Lincoln—who had spent a few years as a lawyer representing Illinois railroad interests—met with a noted Council Bluffs engineer named Granville Dodge. Lincoln wanted Dodge's opinion on the best route.

The Civil War generally shut down railroad construction, other than that associated with the war effort, but Lincoln was so convinced of the importance of a line to California that he pressed both issues. If railroad magnates couldn't do it alone—and certainly there was no chance in the time frame Lincoln had in mind—then the federal government would play a role.

Federal oversight and incentives, bonds and land grants and US army protection, merged with investors and Capitalists, engineers and inventors in a race with huge profits for the winners. The Central Pacific would build from Sacramento east; the Union Pacific from Iowa west. They—the Central Pacific and Union Pacific—would meet at a point to be decided by Congress.

Some historians believe this 2,000 mile stretch across prairie, mountains and desert, started in 1863, could not possibly have been done in six years had it not been for the Civil War. Generals learned through experience to organize men and missions. From the source of supplies to the front lines, co-ordination and timing were as essential as arms and ammunition. Surveyors and engineers and contractors knew how to build railroads before the war. During it, with the power and resources of government behind them, with the future of a nation at stake, they built, repaired, rebuilt, found new and better and faster ways.

When the war ended railroad construction took on additional vigor. Thousands of men either no longer had a home to return to, or simply preferred not to resume their former lives. They had grown accustomed to camp life, were hardened by deprivation and forced marches and, perhaps most importantly for the task ahead, were conditioned to obey orders without question.

In his book, *Nothing Like It In The World,"* Stephen Ambrose suggests this may have been the finest work force ever assembled. They were certainly as diverse. Chinese made a name working for the Central Pacific, Irish did likewise for the Union Pacific. Mormons worked for both, and this was only a part of the representation of ethnicity. Swedes and English and Blacks and Germans and various combinations were part of work crews. Group pictures show traits in common, one of which was physical conditioning. These men carried no fat. They were lean and muscular with work ethic and pride and knew their jobs through repetition. The trans-continental railroad was arguably the world's first assembly line. Men who swung sledges to drive spikes had no other tasks. Neither did those who placed ties. Rail layers and spacers and those who set fishplates, held the spikes, all had their specialty. Three swings of the sledge and the spike was driven, then to the next, three more swings, from early morning until break time and then back at it. They could lay a mile a day, then two miles, and when the going was good, four miles and more. They pushed on, fighting Indians when they had to, an army of their own, supplies and support following on rails just completed.

They were, by all accounts, predominately happy workers. They were well paid and well-taken care of. They slept in box cars modified with bunk beds. A herd of cattle was maintained for beef, and on occasion workers dined on fried chicken, pork chops, or buffalo. Hot cakes and eggs and potatoes for breakfast, boiled beef, potatoes and cabbage at noon, and if the variety wasn't the best there was plenty to eat. They had camaraderie and competition, good food and tobacco, more than enough danger to keep them alert, and on a day off with money in their pockets, Hell on Wheels was not far away.

In the fall of 1867 the Union Pacific portion of the trans-continental railroad was nearing Cheyenne, a route that caused consternation in some quarters as it missed Denver by 100 miles. The benefit of connecting Denver to this coast-to-coast main artery was obvious, and as the UP approached rails were being laid between Cheyenne and Denver, a line that would continue on to the city of Kit Carson in eastern Colorado, and from there to points south and west. Peter Hopley had no trouble finding work.

He arrived at the UP line near Cheyenne as the harsh winter of 1867-68 set in. Grade was primarily done by hand, by men with shovels and wheel barrows, and when the ground froze and snow piled deep grading came to a seasonal halt. Hopley at first worked for his board only. Livestock—horses, mules and hundreds of cattle—had to be taken care of. Hopley was a farm boy. He knew cattle and draft animals and was glad to tend them in exchange for a bunk in a box car and three meals a day. Come spring he was paid $35 a month, he wrote, hauling freight to the western end of the Union Pacific, hard work and risky as well.

Why he left the UP we don't know. He was in the west, hauling freight, for five years (1867 to 1872). The Union Pacific and Central Pacific met in Utah in 1869. Some workers stayed on. Rebuilding track that had been laid more for speed than endurance and safety began almost immediately. Most of the crews, however, broke up and men moved on. Hopley may have been among them, or might have left the UP earlier. Regardless, he went to work on the Cheyenne to Denver route, and when that was done continued as the line was extended on into New Mexico.

He would later write: *"I hauled railroad ties for the Union Pacific extension from Denver to Kit Carson, 150 miles, and fights with Indians were a matter of almost daily occurrence. We lost many a man in those brushes with the reds, for we took desperate chances—chances I would not think of taking today, but we thought little of it then."*

Hopley implies he had no use for the rowdy "Hell on Wheels" menagerie that followed the U.P. Gambling, liquor and women relieved a good many workers of everything they earned. Even legitimate necessities were priced high. Hopley, however, tells us he spent little money and none of it foolishly. He lived off the land, saving nearly all the wages he was paid. There were slack times with the freight and railroad business, mostly weather related, and during these lulls Hopley prospected or found other work. In his memoir, written for the Muffley family history (one of Peter's daughters, Minnie, married Fred Muffley of Idaho), he said that during those five years he drove "everything from a Concord coach to a pack mule."

The Concord coach was a passenger vehicle—not a freighter. It was, in fact, considered to be the finest of stage coaches, the final step in the evolution of multi-passenger, horse-drawn coaches. Wide and tall, elegant yet rugged enough to withstand the roughest of mountain trails, the Concord was the choice of Wells Fargo and other respected stage lines. In his book "Roughing It," published in 1872, Mark Twain called the Concord a "cradle on wheels."

The Concord was normally drawn by four horses. Hopley also drove multi-mule teams. He drove animals harnessed in tandem, drove them in spans four to six wide. There was a skill required; recognizing strengths and weakness in animals, sensing their mood, handling multiple reins and handbrakes and more, sending instructions to lunging beasts through touch and voice in a manner that conveyed confidence and trust, or at least achieved obedience. A good driver, it was said, got the best from a team—a better driver was part of it.

While he'd known draft animals on the farm, worked with them daily, the five-year adventure in Colorado, Wyoming, and New Mexico, gave young Hopley a scope of experience, knowledge, and appreciation for horses he would probably not otherwise have gained.

# Chapter Four

When he returned to Iowa he'd amassed a few hundred dollars (an Atlantic News Telegraph article printed years later put the amount at $3,000), plus, in Hopley's words *"18 yoke of oxen, six wagons and a saddle horse."* He found 80 acres for sale north of Lewis—the price was $25 an acre—and (with brother John co-signing the note) he bought it. The year was 1872.

For the next two years he lived alone, frugally, and farmed his land. In 1874 he married Edna Everly, a Cass County native whose family also came from England.

Peter worked, he said, until he had saved $3,000. With this he and his brother, William, went into partnership on some cattle and did well. While the partnership ended, the brothers owned adjoining parcels of land. They continued to get along well, yet they were competitive.

Peter, even in old age, remembered the teasing he'd taken in school and the vow he'd made to get even by becoming more successful than his tormenters. Success, in his view, was measured in wealth.

The brothers farmed, each wanted to expand, make money, own more land. Both did well.

Shortly after the partnership with his brother terminated, Peter entered into another. We draw the impression that he needed to do so as he had the idea, but not the ready cash. He doesn't tell us who he teamed with. We can speculate that it may have been Oliver Mills. Mills, who was born in the summer of 1821 and died in Lewis in the winter of

1907, had been part of anti-slavery activities with a group that, in all likelihood, included Peter's father. He remained a prominent resident of the community. During his eighty-six years he held several local elective offices. Mills grew comfortably well-to-do through investing, mostly in livestock. If an ambitious young man and family friend, such as Peter Hopley, came around with an idea Oliver Mills was the sort who was willing to listen.

The partnership, whether with Mills or another livestock investor, resulted in the importation of a pair of expensive draft stallions from Canada.

Profiting from this venture, Hopley began buying horses on his own. He evidently made a significant amount of money on cattle as well. His theory was that if a small profit could be derived by feeding a few steers, why not feed a lot of them? He'd seen the growth of ranches in Wyoming and Colorado, had established contacts, and as early as 1877 the newspaper reported that Hopley had "gone west to buy feeder cattle."

In December of 1879 the Telegraph reported that Peter Hopley of Lewis had bought a farm known as the "Ferguson place," which adjoined his. While the acreage wasn't given, the purchase price was reportedly "over $7,000." As Peter had bought his original 80 seven years earlier for $25 an acre, the Ferguson place was probably 240 acres, more or less. He was buying land, and it would be decades before he stopped.

In July of 1884 this article appeared in the Lewis newspaper:

*Peter Hopley is waiting for the arrival of his partner, James Milne, a Scotchman, from whom he received a telegram of Mr. Milne's arrival on this side of the Atlantic with 14 head of horses. He is expected in Lewis later this week.*

Milne also made the news a few weeks later:

*The little Scotchman who showed Peter Hopley's horses at the fair was a dandy. He was raised in a stable and knows all about horses. He showed some Clydesdales that might have broken the record of Maud S.*

(While everything else in the article was likely true, the editor was joking in writing that a Clydesdale could have beaten Maud S. Maud was a racing harness horse, the best of her time. She was all over the news in the mid-1880s when she ran a mile in what was then a world's record. Most any Clydesdale could out-pull her, but would have had no chance in a race.)

During the same summer that Milne came here, Peter Hopley went there. He returned to England—his first trip back since coming to this country twenty-eight years earlier. His purpose was to buy a few select draft animals which would, he gambled, turn a profit. While in Europe he visited his former home in Cheshire, called on relatives, and probably looked up childhood friends. He then went to Scotland (Milne quite likely went with him, but news articles do not so state). There he bought 25 head of Clydesdale horses. Most, if not all, were stallions. The purchase, partly on borrowed money, was a gamble.

He was more than two weeks at sea with, as he put it, "nearly every cent of ready money I had" at risk. He started home with twenty-five tons of high priced horses, and must have thought of the *Black Hawk*. The 1884 crossing with horses went well, however, and he returned to Europe the next year, and the next. Hopley was making money on horses, enough to justify hiring hands to tend his cattle, hogs, and crops while he traveled. And he was always in the market for land.

By the late 1800s Hopley's purchases were making news in Europe. In the fall of 1887 a newspaper in Scotland carried a lengthy article about draft animals purchased *"by Peter Hopley and company for shipment to Lewis, Iowa, County Cass, U.S.A."* The story covered in detail bloodlines of animals and identified sellers, including those with prestigious names such as Cromarty House and the Duke of Hamilton.

> *The French horses are also a fine lot, and were brought to Glasgow for shipment on the Allen Line. Horses like these, should they safely reach their destination, cannot fail to improve the breed in the United States. (Glasgow Herald, October 17, 1887.)*

The reference to safety while in transit was a valid concern. Livestock being transported by train were often damaged. The constant swaying of cars, jolting stops and starts; the sounds and smells and ever-present coal soot combined for a stressful journey. With hogs and cattle an occassional broken leg or a few abrasions were part of the cost of doing business. For these animals the trip was usually one-way. Hopley horses, mostly stallions, some inclined to be excitable, were not going to slaughter. When they traveled by train it was in specially equipped stock cars.

Ships at sea presented additional problems. Train trips were shorter. Sick stock could be unloaded and picked up later. Even on an uneventful crossing in mild weather animals in enclosures below deck were there for three weeks, often longer, subject to the constant rocking, the rise and fall of swells, the conditions that bring about the awful misery of sea-sickness. There was also the problem of fresh air. Ships of the time were notorious for stale and stagnant below-deck air, a conditioned worsened by animal excretions.

Storms at sea could throw a one-ton horse, already nervous and sick, from its feet or against a wall. A horse on a rope could become entangled. Broken necks were uncommon, but not unheard of.

Hopley's horse-buying expeditions to the continent became routine. To accommodate stock he built a barn with stables not far from the depot in Lewis. An 1889 article in the Telegraph describes it as being part of *"the horse buying and breeding business of Peter Hopley & Co., one of the largest operations of the kind in the entire west. He has just returned from Europe with a cargo of 44 horses. He makes two trips a year."*

Although Hopley does not tell of losses, he must have had some. By the mid-1890s he was taking special precautions. He tried to get animals on the ship early to accustom them to their surroundings and the motion of waves. Hopley-owned horses were placed in individual stalls. The walls were padded. Fresh bedding was applied as needed. Peter tended them personally and, although he wasn't a veterinarian, he had an abundance of practical knowledge.

At a time when the draft horse powered American agriculture, Peter Hopley became—if newspaper accounts are to be believed—one of this nation's leading importers and breeders of blooded animals. He liked horses and knew them. Five years as a teamster in the west had helped make him a keen judge of horses; when he went buying he knew what he was looking for.

Hopley did not limit his purchases to a particular breed. Clydesdales comprised his first shipment. Folklore has it that a major brewery, noted for their Clydesdales, bought from Hopley. They could have chosen Percheron or Shire or Belgian. Hopley, dealing in animals that would work, bought and sold them all.

He understood that draft horses of Europe were superior to stock in America. Specialized breeds were developed when knighthood was a way of life, when horses were owned by royalty with time and money. Their horses had been improved by selective breeding, by daily use on European farms for centuries. Fine animals were, of course, brought to Colonial America. But because of cost and availability they were cross-bred with what was here. European blood-lines were, in this country, rapidly diluted.

If Hopley had a personal favorite, an article in a 1913 newspaper (the Telegraph) indicates that breed was the "Suffolk Punch." Developed in the 16th century in Suffolk County in Hopley's native England, these horses stood nearly six foot at the shoulder and weighed, in trim working condition, 2,000 pounds or a bit more. Although popular in much of England, their numbers were limited. A mare would bear only a few foals during her lifetime; each of which reduced her time in the field. Stallions were often not easy-keepers. Farmers, for the most part, were more likely to raise animals for replacement than sale. Belgian and French horses were more numerous, easier to acquire. More of them were shipped to the U.S., making them better known and more in demand. Hopley, though, liked his Suffolk horses and bought them when he could.

The Morgan and Standardbred, the latter developed in this country, were the horse of choice for lightweight buggies and carriages. Hopley had a few, but his business dealings were in bigger animals. The Suffolk Punch had the strength and bulk to pull farm implements. They were also agile. While any of the breeds he imported could work the field, be ridden or pull a fire truck or beer wagon, Hopley told an inquiring newspaper reporter he thought the Suffolk Punch was the better all-purpose animal. Harry, his oldest son, came to prefer Belgians. The Punch, though, remained the draft animals of choice while Peter was making the decisions.

To acquire the kind of stock he wanted, Hopley traveled into Scotland, Germany, and France. He scoured the English countryside for the Suffolk Punch. When he found a good source he returned year after year. Sellers who had what he wanted received a fair price—in cash. They were likely to exchange letters during the year, and have a good colt or two when Hopley made the next trip.

While Hopley made money on horses, he wrote later that if he had it to do over again he "*would not take up this branch of business.*" He'd have done better financially, in his view, had he by-passed horses and focused on cattle, sheep, and hogs. He'd been right often enough on markets to believe he could gauge them with a degree of accuracy and "*I would go in more for speculative live-stock farming, feeding to the market, and so on.*" His oldest son, Harry, would one day take that advice.

In all likelihood his overseas excursions, once he'd become financially independent, were less about business and more about satisfying his yearn to travel.

"*Folks often say to me: Hopley, you had exceptional opportunities. You came here when the country was young and land cheap. You got in on the ground floor. Of course you worked hard, but you were lucky. What could you do nowadays? What would you do if you were a young man, poor and without your present experience? You couldn't make it.*"

Of these skeptics Hopley wrote: "*They make me tired. If I were a young man again—twenty-five or thirty—and had my wife here with me, I'd make good again. Here is how I would do it. I would hire out as a farmhand. I would get $50 a month, for that is the wages of our hands and they are not as good a men as I was. But that is not all. I would get a house to live in and fuel. I would get a garden, chickens, and the cow. At the end of the year I would have earned $600, and I would have every cent of that $600. I would have fed the family and kept ourselves on the products of the garden, the chickens, and the cow. I would work another year. By that time I would have earned $1,200. I will allow $200 for unforeseen and unavoidable expense. I would have $1,000 left. But that is only half the story. By that time I would have a credit of $1,000 to*

*$1,500, because the banker would know me, would know I was a hard worker and good saver. He would see me coming in every month with my pay check. He would look at my account and see I was not drawing out any money. Believe me, the banker soon gets to know who deserves to get ahead, who is worthy of credit."*

Hopley distinguishes himself from many successful men of his time by frequent references to his wife. It is not unusual to read memoirs written by gentlemen of that era and find little or no mention of their spouse. While these may have been loving and appreciative husbands, women took a back seat. They had their role; men theirs. Men were at the forefront, and men took the credit—or the blame. Peter Hopley routinely recognizes Edna as a partner in his success, tells us she worked as hard as he did, that if he were to begin again his wife would be a necessary partner.

Hopley went on to write that if starting anew he'd rent a small farm, buy used machinery and inexpensive horses, that his wife would work equally hard. They'd save money. They'd buy a few cows, hogs and sheep, raise all their own food. *"We'd be up with the sun and we'd work all day. After a while I'd go to the banker again and say: Mr. Banker, I've got so much ready money. I have so much stock. I owe so much. I want to go over to Omaha and buy some feeders. There's good money in it. And Mr. Banker would be glad to lend me the money to buy those cattle. He'd know I was paying my store bills, that my wife wasn't wasting money, that we were working and saving, and deserved to succeed. In ten years I'd have a good stake. That's how I'd start again."*

This was easy advice to give as it was exactly how, in his words, he'd "made myself a millionaire." He worked, saved, invested, leveraged his capital, and spent nothing on frivolities. Or so he said.

Forty years after Peter Hopley wrote those lines on the virtues of hard work and clean living one of his grandsons was sitting in a Spencer steak house. "Hickory" Hopley was spending a few days at the Clay County fairgrounds where Angus cattle from the famed Hopley herd were being shown. He tossed down several double scotches, building on a drunk he'd worked on most of the day. His way of ordering a drink was to tap an empty glass with a spoon, creating an annoying and increasingly louder noise until a waitress, as likely to be groped as tipped, responded.

The boorish behavior he'd displayed was only the beginning. Hopley surveyed the crowd of diners. Most, including young families and elderly couples, were quietly enjoying their dinner. Hickory stood. At six-foot one and burly, he commanded attention.

"Let's fight!" he shouted, "or f---! I don't care which, but let's get something going! It's too God-damned quiet in here!"

# Chapter Five

Peter Hopley's reputation as an evaluator and dealer in livestock attracted the attention of William Cody. As Peter's grandsons told the story, he and Buffalo Bill met in the late 1860s while both were working for the railroad. This may be true, as both were in the same area at the same time and their paths may have crossed.

Buffalo Bill was, in the early 1900s, touring this country and Europe with his Wild West Show. An Iowa native, he made several appearances in southwest Iowa, drawing—according to news reports—as many as 10,000 to 12,000 people per performance. His cowboys and Indians, stagecoaches, cavalry and simulated trail drives, combined to require scores of animals. Cody and his herdsman were constantly in the market for good replacement stock. Hopley proved to be a reliable source. They did business and, according to newspaper accounts, became personal friends. An article published in the Atlantic News Telegraph after Hopley's death states that Cody and Hopley made a few horse-buying trips to Europe together.

(This probably didn't happen. Articles about these overseas trips, regularly published upon his return, tell of numerous friends and family members who accompanied him. We find no reference to Cody doing so. More likely, given the fact that Cody's Wild West show was so popular in Europe, the two men met and renewed their friendship while buying horses abroad. If they crossed the Atlantic together it was probably a coincidence.)

Hopley's livestock business would eventually be facilitated by what was called the "Hopley Switch." He was a man with a high regard for railroads. While he'd earned part of the stake used to buy land by working for one, his appreciation began even earlier. As a boy he helped his father raise wheat, corn and livestock. He wrote that grain crops were ground at the mill in Lewis or, in the case of sorghum, converted to syrup on the farm. Hogs were raised to feed the family. What was produced on the farm was mostly consumed there. For the most part markets were either non-existent or inaccessible. There was a buyer and seller, sometimes, in St. Joseph and another in Council Bluffs, but getting there in a horse-drawn wagon, with little for roads and less for bridges, was a problem. Returning with a load was more difficult.

When it was necessary to buy grain, Hopley later recalled, the price was set by the seller, if one could be found. Money was so scarce it was common to barter; to trade something of equal value or, more often, to exchange goods for labor. Peter was a young man when the railroad began operations in Cass County. The benefits, he noted, were immediate and remarkable. Grain elevators were built. Surplus crops could be sold for money, and If buyers didn't offer a fair price grain could be shipped, at a reasonable cost, elsewhere.

During the first few years Peter and Edna farmed they drove livestock to the Rock Island depot in Atlantic, which connected with big-city markets in Omaha. Thirty-five miles to the south, Montgomery County was served by the Chicago, Burlington & Quincy (CB&Q). Getting to points east and west was not a problem; north and south was another matter. A good many area residents wanted a line connecting the Rock Island in Atlantic with the CB&Q in Red Oak, then extending on to Shenandoah and St. Joseph to the south. From Atlantic the route was projected to Audubon and beyond.

Neither the CB&Q nor the Rock Island was anxious to do this. A Montgomery County history, written by W.W. Merritt, who was present at the time, tells us a disgruntled group of local investors—both in Atlantic and Red Oak—began trying to raise capital to build and operate their own railroad. Whether they'd have succeeded is unknown. According to Merritt, the two major railroads, not wanting competition, were moved by the threat to do the job themselves. Their agreement had the CB&Q building north, creating the depot town of Elliott. The Rock Island extended south, brushing the west edge of the existing town of Lewis, to the "roundhouse" turn-around point in Griswold—a town created for that purpose.

This took place in 1879. Lewis merchants on the original town square, seven blocks east of the new depot, either moved closer or, eventually, closed. While it remained one town, for a few years residents referred to "east Lewis" and "west Lewis." Hopley acquired a lot at the corner of block 69, the junction of California and Webster Streets, and built the barn previously referred to. (He built a lot of barns, probably a dozen or more. Some were in Lewis, others on his farms. At least a couple of them burned and were replaced. When papers write of "the barn on the Hopley place" it is not always possible to know which barn is being referred to.)

The location at the corner of California and Webster served well, being near his home, just a block off Main Street, and not far from the depot. For several years livestock was driven from the farm to the barn and adjoining corrals to be held pending shipment, or from the depot to barn to be fed and watered before driving to the farm.

This arrangement was better than herding stock to Atlantic, and was improved even more a few years later. Hopley, ever expanding, owned land north of Lewis that bordered the track on both sides. By the mid-1880s he was well-to-do and well-connected. He also shipped a lot of livestock. In the fall of 1902 this article appeared in the Lewis Standard:

> *Peter Hopley now has over 900 head of cattle on his ranch north of town. Most of them are white faces and the best the west produces. He has just had a switch completed up at his ranch and will hereafter load and unload stock on his ranch.*

How much convincing he had to do we don't know—perhaps none— but the railroad did for him something that was generally reserved for manufacturers, stockyards, and grain elevators. They built the Hopley Switch. Hopley erected the corrals. When Peter scheduled a shipment out the Rock Island left the requested number of boxcars. Not many farmers could routinely fill a car with either fat cattle or hogs. Hopley sent several at a time, often making the trip to Chicago in a very nicely appointed caboose.

Bob Kennedy, old enough to remember seeing the Hopley Switch, says it was located near where the rodeo arena was later built. This would put it 100 yards or so northwest of what became the Hopco truck stop. Others we interviewed are of the opinion it was farther south. Highway 6, as it runs between Lewis and Atlantic, had not yet been built.)

The barn in Lewis, a holding point for Hopley stock being shipped by rail, was no longer needed for that purpose. Hopley may have sold grain and hay there prior to the coming of his Hopley Switch; after that he converted the barn into a full-time livery.

In the 1947 interview with Simpson, Wayland Hopley says members of the family, in the early days of Lewis, were involved with a stage coach line and hotel. While this may be true, we find no record of either. The barn was used for various purposes, but was built well after stage coach travel through Lewis was discontinued. Peter seems to have driven all manner of conveyances while in the west, including a Concord stagecoach, so his stories of that may be what Wayland had heard.

A few days after completion of the Switch an unfortunate occurrence took place nearby. From the Lewis Standard:

*A sad accident took place up at Peter Hopley's ranch north of town on Wednesday afternoon. The sons of some of the hired men were trying to kill a skunk which had taken refuge in a tree when in some manner the little son of L.B. Focht was accidently shot in the cheek by one of the other boys. The rifle ball severed the jugular vein in his neck and passed around to the base of the skull. He suffered a great loss of blood before the doctor arrived. All that was possible was done for him, but the little fellow died in great agony at four o'clock in the afternoon. Although hunting has its allurements, a number of accidents have resulted from the sport around the state in the past few months, some of which were fatal.*

There were other fatal accidents. A Lewis man named Sherman Jackson was a hired hand on Peter Hopley's farm during the early 1890s. He left for employment elsewhere. In 1898 he married a daughter of William Meredith, a prominent and well-to-do resident of Lewis. In the spring of 1900 Hopley asked the young man to return, offering him a job as foreman. Jackson accepted. Five months later, on an August day with dark clouds boiling and a storm moving in, he and two hired men set out to repair fences. Jackson was riding on the back of the wagon while D.D. Brainard and Andrew Christensen were on the driver's seat. A bolt of lightning struck Jackson, killing him instantly and, according to the news account, leaving his body *"badly burned and disfigured."* The team of horses pulling the wagon were also killed. Inexplicably, the two men between Jackson and the horses were not injured.

The same edition of the paper that reported the death of the Focht boy informed readers that Mrs. Peter Hopley was ill. A few days later she was reported to be suffering from pneumonia. Her husband arranged for a private nurse from Des Moines to care for her in the home.

The Hopley Switch was used regularly. An example of the care used in transporting horses, and reference to their value, is found in the following article, taken from the Atlantic Democrat of October 25, 1907:

*Are the Best on Earth*

*Peter Hopley, accompanied by his son, Harry, arrived from the east last night, having in charge two carloads of horses— the pick of the best stables in Belgium, France, Germany and England. There were thirty horses in the shipment and include the finest strains of Percherons, Shires, German Coaches, Suffolk and French Coach horses that are the best money could buy. It is the most varied and best installations made on the Hopley farm of blooded horses, and it is doubtless one of the largest shipments made by any Iowa importer in recent years.*

*The voyage across the Atlantic was made without mishap, and the trip from New York was equally free of any injury to animals. They were most comfortably transported in a couple of special horse cars which had every modern convenience for the safe transportation of horses whose value would run into the thousands. The cars were heated by steam and lighted by gas. The stalls were well cushioned. It would be almost impossible for a horse to be injured in one of these modern conveniences.*

*One of the branch engines made a special trip down the south line last night with the two cars and the horses arrived safe and sound at the Hopley farm.*

Hopley had his barn in town, more of them on his farms, but traveling as he did offered an opportunity to stroll through the best. He liked the barns he saw in Europe, used them as a model for plans he drew himself, then hired a local carpenter named Hedges to do the work. In May of 1905 the following article appeared in the Telegraph:

*J.S. Hedges has just completed the large barn he has been building for Peter Hopley on his horse ranch between this city and Lewis. It has been built after plans prepared by Mr. Hopley, who has seen the best barns in the United States, England and Scotland, and he says his may be the best he has ever seen. When Mr. Hedges called a halt last Saturday Mr. Hopley was perfectly satisfied, and Jim says he is very proud of his job.*

This barn was on land Peter Hopley owned on the White Pole Road in Section 26, Washington Township, probably not far from the home later built for Wayland and Helen. The latter house, at 60131 585th Street, is still occupied. The barn no longer exists.

The same paper tells us William's daughter, Jennie, then living in Avoca, spent Sunday in Lewis and Atlantic visiting friends and relatives. She may have stopped by to see her uncle and his new barn.

Another barn, similar to the one Hedges completed in 1905, was put up by Peter and Edna's oldest son, Harry, on his West Side Farm. It remains the site of countless memories—very few who visited or worked there forgot that impressive barn. Dale Roush, whose father was a long-time employee of Hopley, spent much of his youth on the farm. He remembers climbing into the loft with a friend, finding a buggy there, and taking turns pulling each other around. Tom Pope, born in 1933 on a farm nearby, recalls catching pigeons in the same loft. He remembers the horse stalls; fine stalls with floor to ceiling walls and massive doors. Each door had an opening through which a horse could extend its head and have a look around. These openings, Pope said, were later equipped with bars. The reason, according to him, was that during World War ll German POWs worked on Hopley farm. Their sleeping quarters were the stalls, and bars installed for that reason. (More on this later. Pope was right about the bars and the prisoners. Wayland Hopley's experiment with low-cost labor, however, did not work out well.)

Growth led to changes in terminology. Newspapers for years referred to the Peter Hopley farm, which he called "Riverside Farm," as just that. As noted in the article above the place became the "Hopley Ranch." "Hopley Switch" was, by the 1920s, called by newspapers "Hopley Station." It wasn't quite a depot, but there was considerable activity. When what is now Highway 6 was paved across southwest Iowa the grounds adjoining the siding was used, by the construction company of McKinkle and Kileen, for storage and parking. Machinery and material shipped by rail for road work was sent to Hopley's. Part of the project of paving the stretch of road between Atlantic and the Pottawattamie County line was, according to a June 30, 1930 article in the Telegraph, paving the road from the highway to "Hopley's Station."

Hopley's secret to success, he wrote time and again, was no secret at all. *"Let me tell you one thing: the first ten years of our married life my wife and I worked hard as human beings ever worked. Corn was worth practically nothing. I have sold as good a hogs as ever went to market for two cents a pound. We raised a large family. In ten years, with the low prevailing prices, we accumulated $30,000 over and above all our expenses. I could do it again, too, and do it better still. When you come right down to it, hard work and frugality are the only secrets of success. There is no other way under the sun. It doesn't matter what you do, hard work, connected with an ability to run your business, will succeed."*

He must have had a strained relationship with at least some of his hired hands. Hopley had to have them. He could not have farmed more than one or two hundred acres without. He could work day and night, so could his wife and sons and daughters, but horse-drawn machinery can cover only so much ground. Corn was planted and cultivated one or two rows at a time. It was picked by hand, unloaded with a scoop shovel. There were no milking machines. As Hopley bought more land he had no choice but to hire more men. Houses on farms he acquired were occupied by employees, as were several small homes built on or near the original eighty-acre place. Hopley had himself labored long and hard. He expected hired men to do likewise. He makes no secret of his feeling that they were overpaid, that he was a better man than any of them.

*"The average hired man of today is a conundrum to me. I can't understand him. Farm labor is the highest priced unskilled labor in the world. I figure that a man who is paid $50 a month on our place is getting $100, counting rent, fuel, chickens, and so on. Almost everything that he eats is raised on the place and costs him nothing. The average man in town earns $2.50 or $3.00 a day, and he doesn't work every day. He must pay for every bit of food he eats. How much better off, therefore, the farmhand is! What we need is a revival of the good, old-fashioned ideas that a man must work and save, that energy, ambition, and nerve are what make men rich, and nothing else."*

The reference to $50 monthly salaries shows that wages had gone up. In an October, 1907 article in an Atlantic newspaper called the Farm Messenger we read that Bob Roush of Lewis had taken a job at the Hopley farm and would draw $35 a month. (We might question the reported $35 monthly salary, as census records from 1915 shows Bob Roush having an annual income of $200. Census takers were not always told the truth.)

Bob Roush got a raise, probably several of them. He was twenty-three years of age when Peter hired him. As much of the help was seasonal, we don't know if Roush was full time from the beginning, but he was later. Between 1907 and 1955 when, at the age of seventy-one, he retired and moved back to Lewis, he worked for Peter, then Harry, then Wayland. For most of those years he fed cattle. He no doubt plowed, planted corn, cultivated and made hay at one time. Later, we are told, he did not. Neither did he fix fences, paint buildings, tend hogs or spread manure. Bob Roush fed cattle. This was a job any of the hired hands could do, but doing it right was another matter. Knowing what to feed and when to make adjustments, recognizing when something was not right and spotting the problem early, knowing which were prime for market and which were not, all this took ability and Bob Roush had it.

Tom Pope, while spending his early years on a farm near the Hopley place, liked to watch Roush do his work. "They always fed with a team of horses and a wagon. I used to ride along. He'd start early in the morning, hitching the team and driving to a silo, then climbing inside and scooping out silage. Then he'd drive to a grain bin and shovel on corn and when the wagon was full he'd start scooping into feed bunks." There were so many cattle that Bob Roush spent all day feeding them. Using different rations for separate corrals of cattle in different stages of fattening, he'd empty the wagon and refill, feed and go back for more. By about noon he'd made the round, finished the morning feeding. After dinner he'd hitch to a different team and start over. The horses, Tom thinks, were either Belgian or Percheron.

Whichever the breed, the animals impressed Bob's youngest son, Dale Roush. "They knew the routine, were well trained. As a small boy I'd be on the seat holding the reins and pretend I was driving them. I wasn't, of course. They paid me no attention. But I thought I was, and it was fun." Bob would open a gate and the horses would pass through, stopping without a command. With Roush in the wagon scooping corn the horses needed only a word to start, stop, and they handled mud better than a tractor. Bob Roush drove horses and shoveled corn on Hopley farms for nearly four decades.

Roush was thirty-three when, in 1917, he married nineteen-year-old Beatrice Doty. All four of their children were born while the family lived in a tenet house on Hopley Farms. "They treated us good," Dale said, "and dad thought highly of them. He wasn't paid much, I suppose, but we had a house to live in and a garden and every time they'd butcher we'd get quite a bit of meat."

Although Hopley attended country school for only a part of one winter as a child, and the school in Lewis for less than two days, his writing is that of an educated man. *The Iowa Homestead* was a popular magazine in the Midwest, one that later combined with a publication operated by Henry Wallace. It was, for a time, known as *Iowa Homestead and Wallace's Farmer,* later just as *Wallace's Farmer.* Articles were solicited from those who had experience in agriculture and had done well. Hopley contributed. His emphasis on hard work and frugality may have grown repetitive. He tells the reader he does not wish to sound boastful, then sounds boastful. Still, his articles on crop production and animal husbandry were informative and well received. He was invited to do more.

He and Edna's first three children were girls; Beulah, Margaret and Edith. Harry was born in 1881. He was followed by Edna, then the twins, Minnie and Mary, and Gertrude. The youngest was Wayland Arrowsmith, born in 1894.

Edna and Peter were loving parents. He liked to take one or more of his children to the field, to town, on rides in the carriage. For a span of thirty years he went to Europe; usually once a year but sometimes twice. Virtually all his trips rated mention in local newspapers. We found no articles telling us he went alone. Edna went at times, although as years passed and her bouts of illness increased, she went less frequently. While everyone in the family had chances to go, Harry, the eldest son, made the journey more often than his siblings. His range of life experiences would not approach that of his father, but Harry grew up around horses and cattle and acquired a wealth of knowledge. He would become a major producer of hogs and highly regarded as both an exhibitor and judge of cattle and horses.

As Peter's family grew, so did his net worth. Any time nearby land was offered for sale—particularly that adjoining what he already owned—he was a potential buyer. A local joke was that Peter Hopley didn't want all the land in the county; only what bordered his.

By the turn of the century he'd amassed nearly 2,000 acres and was in the market for more. His was a huge farm at a time when it was common for a family to exist on eighty acres. Values throughout his lifetime rose steadily. His father bought for $1.25 an acre. Peter's first farm cost him $25 an acre. By the early 1900s good farmland was bringing $150 an acre. That, Hopley wrote, was a ceiling. He stopped buying Iowa land. He bought elsewhere, though, and told his sons that Iowa property, even as the average price passed $200 an acre, remained a bargain for a young man.

He bought building lots in Lewis at various times. An 1880s listing of town business places includes the "Hopley store." While this is probably the barn on Webster street, one that was also called the "Hopley Feed and Stallion Barn," at one time a waypoint between his farm and depot (and later a livery stable), it might have been yet another endeavor. Hopley was buying, selling, building and converting at a pace that was probably difficult for newspapers to keep up with.

He purchased property in California, owned a half section of ranchland in Nebraska. We find newspaper references to land in Montana. The following appeared in the News Telegraph on February 29, 1900:

> *Peter Hopley of Lewis returned this morning from Phoenix, Arizona, from whither he had gone to sell some real estate belonging to him in that state.*

This item is noteworthy, as it offers a glimpse of Peter Hopley that neither news articles nor his own writing provides. A story handed down in the family has him being a serious poker player. He may have been a good one, either learning the game or refining his skills while hauling freight in the frontier west. A previously referred to piece in the News Telegraph, which is consistent with others derived from Hopley interviews, has him returning from his Colorado adventures with $3000, plus a wagon and considerable livestock. In his "How I Became a Millionaire" essay he tells of working for $35 a month. While there might have been months he made more, there were also times when Rocky Mountain weather shut down the freight business. There was time to play cards and little else to do. He had no income as a teamster during extended winter periods. Had he averaged $35 per month, every month, and saved every penny he would, in the five years he was there, have accumulated but $2100. Did he perhaps find a little gold? If so he'd probably have been proud enough of to have made mention. Instead he wrote that he found none. Poker seems more likely, particularly if a story told by Wayland and Harry is true.

Gambling was, after all, part of Peter's life. Planting a crop is a gamble. Playing the markets as he did a bigger one. Of the era in which Peter Hopley thrived, Mark Twain wrote: *"Everyone was out to get rich; dishonestly if they could, honestly if they had to."* Peter Hopley did not amass his fortune dishonestly, but Twain's observation affords a view of the time in which he lived. Gambling was commonplace. Cowboys and freight haulers anted up. The wealthy enjoyed the same games, just for higher stakes. The people Peter Hopley met and the places he went offered endless opportunities to toss in a few dollars and cut the deck.

Hopley, his sons said, won some Arizona land in a card game. He walked away with the deed to a parcel in or near Phoenix. Harry and Wayland are said to have later lamented the fact that Peter sold when he did. Land in the Phoenix area was soon to skyrocket in value. His sons felt Peter, in this particular instance, folded when he should have held.

To every side there are at least two stories. An article carried in the Lewis newspaper in July of 1892 offers this one: *"Peter Hopley, recently returned from a trip to Arizona, was so pleased with land along the Salt River near Phoenix that he invested considerable money in real estate there."*

Make of this what you will. He may have bought the land and the poker game didn't happen. Then again, the poker story may be true and he chose to tell a reporter something else. Another possibility is that both versions are true. He was traveling, spending, speculating, buying and selling at the time to the extent that it would have been feasible for him to have bought land in the afternoon, played cards and won more another day—or maybe even the same.

At the time he wrote of having made in excess of one million dollars, he had several good years still ahead. To grasp his worth consider that a working man then might earn $600 or $700 a year. Today a comparable laborer makes at least $25,000, or 35 times as much. A dollar in the 1890s equaled about $40 today. Most of Hopley's assets, however, were not in dollars; they were in land. Much of that land is now worth 200 times, or more, than what he paid. We cannot even guess at what the property in Phoenix might be worth. His real estate holdings in California would be of enormous value.

All this makes Hopley's first million, given that the bulk of it was in real estate, impossible to precisely evaluate in today's dollars. $50 million does not seem unreasonable, and is probably conservative.

He bought, in 1884, two adjoining parcels of land in Lewis (legally described as lot 1, blocks 21 and 22 in the Southside addition of

Dickerson's Addition). Shortly thereafter he set about building what would come to be known as the "Hopley mansion."

When we think of "pioneer women" we tend to envision dirt-floor cabins, a steady diet of corn mush and salt pork, deprivation and disease, toil and trouble. Edna Everly, born in Cass County years before Atlantic, Griswold, and other railroad towns existed, was a bona fide "pioneer woman." In 1855, the year of her birth, most dwellings in the area were primitive log cabins. Only scattered plots of sod had been broken. Her early years were spent in the most humble surroundings. When her obituary refers to her as a "true pioneer" there can be no argument.

She had other crosses to bear. Edna barely knew her father, and probably remembered little of her mother. Joseph Everly was born in Ohio in 1821 and married Caroline Jones in Indiana in 1843. A few years later they moved to Cass County, Iowa, living for a time in a primitive cabin near Iranistan. They bought and relocated to an 80 acre farm north of Lewis (section 26 of Washington Township, land that Peter Hopley would later own). Caroline and Joseph had several children, of which Edna was the youngest. Caroline, according to an entry in the 1884 Cass County History died, but no date is given and we find no obituary or death certificate. Whatever the fate of Caroline, in May of 1859, when Edna was four, Joseph married Adelia Page. She was then a 19-year-old school teacher. Everly's first-born child was but three years younger than the bride.

Joe Everly was a drinker, and a bad one. This was exhibited while he was spending time in the rowdy, hell-raising, whiskey-flowing hangouts in Iranistan, and continued when activities of this type moved to Lewis. He was said to be a genial fellow and good neighbor when sober. When Joseph Everly drank he was a different, and disagreeable, person. Whether he abused his children or either of his wives we don't know, but he was the type. Accounts of his death say he became quarrelsome when under the influence. According to the "Memoirs of Thomas Meridith," published in the Cass County Biographies section of the 1884 county history, such was the case on a September night in 1860.

Meredith wrote that Adelia Page was the first school teacher in the county, then continues: *"Joseph Everly, her husband, was a clever man and good neighbor, but he was a fool when he got drunk, which he would do when he went to Iranistan. He and Jake Watson went home together on a sled, as they lived at that time on the river a few miles north of Lewis. Everly was killed on the way home and his body found the next day. Jake, fearing trouble, went away for a while and then came back and nothing was done about it. It was a drunken freak and the people thought that if he got drunk and wanted to whip everybody he ought to be killed."*

Another version is found in a biographical section of rootsweb. *"Joseph Everly was a man who bore a good reputation when in his normal condition but who, unfortunately, was addicted to the excessive use of liquor. One day, in the fall of 1860, he rode into Lewis on horseback and spent a good portion of the day in drinking. Jacob Watson was also in town that day with a team and, about dusk, upon finishing his trading, started home. It seems that after having passed Turkey Creek bridge, Watson was overtaken by Everly and a quarrel began which was overheard by a neighboring family. The next morning Everly was found dead in the brush at the side of the road three quarters of a mile north of Turkey Creek bridge with the marks of a club across his skull. The affair did not create much excitement. The grand jury took the matter in hand, but did not issue an indictment against anyone and the matter was dropped. Everly is buried at the Lewis cemetery."*

The latter of the two versions is more likely the correct one. There was an altogether different incident near Iranistan involving two men on a sled in bitter cold weather, and it seems likely Meredith got this mixed up with the Everly killing. We say this as Watson and Everly were not likely to be sharing a sled, especially in mid-September. By 1860 Iranistan had largely faded away, and even if it had not Lewis was much closer to both the Watson and Everly homes.

Both versions end the same, and offer a similar view of Edna Everly's father. She was taken in by neighbors, Brigley and Martha Macomber, and lived with them until her marriage to Peter Hopley.

# Chapter Six

Of Edna Hopley, her husband wrote: *"The first ten years of our married life my wife and I worked hard, as hard as human beings ever worked."* He was saving nearly every dime they earned, investing, determined to do more than just get by. Edna, in the early years, had no frills. Yet, just a decade after marriage, her life-style underwent radical changes.

These pioneer women were perfectly capable of adapting. When Edna Hopley acquired wealth, she was not shy about distributing it for the enjoyment of herself and family.

By the late 1880s she was making the social news on a regular basis. Peter had his life, Edna had hers. She belonged to societies, groups, and women's clubs. Her great-grandfather, Leonard Everly, had served in the Revolutionary War. This gave Edna eligibility for the Daughters of the American Revolution. Patriotism ran high in the 1880s and 90s, and Edna's membership in the DAR was of itself enough to give her an elevated social status.

She entertained, and was entertained by, a circle of regulars. She and Peter could together enjoy Buffalo Bill's show and concerts in the Lewis city park. They took family outings, enjoyed picnics and bathing and special events at Crystal Lake south of Lewis. Peter, though, was away a good deal; increasingly so as time passed. Edna sometimes traveled with him, but not often on business trips. When he was away his absence did not keep her home. She enjoyed the Chautauqua. We find frequent news items telling of Mrs. Peter Hopley, accompanied by one or more of her many lady friends, and later her daughters, traveling to Council Bluffs or Des Moines to shop or take in a theater performance.

She spent time with her garden and flowers. She enjoyed visitors. The following two items appeared in the Atlantic Telegraph on July 8, 1890.

> *Mrs. Peter Hopley and Mrs. W.J. Harris have returned from the Chautauqua in Council Bluffs.*

Edna's traveling companion was also a noteworthy woman. William J. Harris was born in Pennsylvania in 1842, married, and he and Lucy came to Iowa just before the Civil War. He enlisted in Poweshiek County, fought in several engagements, made sergeant, then was taken prisoner. Upon release at the end of the war he and Lucy moved to Lewis. They made their home on Webster Street, less than a block from where Peter and Edna built their mansion. A news article in 1889 describes a water well being dug jointly by Harris and Peter Hopley, one that would be equipped with a windmill and water tower holding several hundred barrels. A system of underground piping was completed in the fall of that year which provided an ample supply of water to the Hopley and Harris homes, as well as the barn and stable each had in the back yard. Harris was listed in the census at about that time as a grain dealer. Later, after the Cass County Bank of Lewis had failed, it was re-opened under the directorship of several men, including Hopley and Harris. By 1910 W.J. Harris was president of that bank. He retired in the late 19-teens and he and Lucy moved to Long Beach, California. Peter, in later years, often visited their California home during the winter months.

After telling of a birth, a social gathering, and other unrelated matters, the same column that told of Mrs. Hopley and Mrs. Harris attending a Chautauqua performance offers this item:

> *Mrs. Peter Hopley invited her many friends to her commodious residence to witness the rare sight of a night blooming cereus in full bloom. About fifty guests admired the delicate beauty of this rare flower.*

The blooming of the cereus was a newsworthy happening. Sometimes called "Queen of the Night," it remains a rare flower. The plant, an unusual cactus, is native to Mexico. The white, fragrant blossoms, which can be up to a foot in diameter, grow as buds for weeks before bursting forth late at night. By dawn they are gone.

A gathering of fifty ladies in the elegant gardens adjoining a home as imposing as the Hopley mansion in Lewis, there in the darkness to witness the blooming of a flower native to Mexico, was an eminently reportable event—and a sharp contrast to what Edna's life had been just a few years before.

(A lady who would have enjoyed Edna's garden was Eudora Welty, a native of Mississippi. Ms. Welty grew up watching her mother lavish care on her cereus plants, anticipating the night of the bloom. Eudora was, in the 1930s, a well-known writer. She organized a club dedicated to the propagation of her favorite plant. The club's motto, "Don't take it cereus, life's too mysterious," would probably have been to Edna Hopley's liking.)

As the years passed Edna's social calendar increasingly included her daughters.

*"Mrs. Hopley and daughter, Edith, returned after spending several days at the state fair, where cattle and horses from the Hopley farm are being shown."* A few weeks later: *"Mrs. Hopley and daughters are soon to leave for the south, where they will spend several weeks."*

*"Mrs. Hopley and the twins, Minnie and Mary, departed this morning for Des Moines."*

Members of the Hopley family helped see in the New Year on the evening of December 31, 1913. The related article reads, in part:

*Between three and four hundred people who attended the Charity Ball in the Masonic Temple agreed that the ball was the most brilliant social affair ever held in this city and the best time they had enjoyed for many a day. Of these facts the ladies in the receiving line were assured as guests passed out at the close of the ball. There were none on the entire list of those present who did not enjoy themselves and the New Year's spirit. The grand march was an imposing procession and the line of the march extended twice around the large Masonic hall ballroom.*

*The dance hall was beautifully adorned with festoons of green and white draped from different parts of the hall to the pillars with a profusion of tinsel making the lighting effect very beautiful. The program was just as published before with the exception of the solo by Miss Edith O'Connell whose place was taken by Miss Averil Faulkner of Des Moines as Miss O'Connell was unable to sing due to a bad cold.*

Other soloists followed, accompanied by the Atlantic Concert Orchestra Band.

While the sentence that included the phrase *"as guests passed out at the close of the ball"* was probably nothing more than a poor choice of words, the article went on to refer to a *"frappe bowl filled with delicious drink."* The evening was one of merrymaking, music, dancing, toasts and high spirits.

Certain ladies were cited for their exquisite evening gowns. Among them was Mrs. Peter Hopley who wore *"a purple velvet gown with gold trimmings."* Also elegantly dressed were Mrs. Frank Lumsden of Red Oak (Peter and Edna's daughter, Margaret) and Mrs. Harry Hopley of Lewis. Wayland Hopley, then nineteen and in his first year of college, was home for the holidays. He attended the ball. If he had a date the article neglected to so mention.

A few evenings earlier Mrs. Hopley had entertained guests in her home with a fine oyster supper. She did so again, with a change in menu, a few days later.

The gala events of the 1913 holiday season ushered in a typically eventful, if not entirely pleasant, year for the Hopleys of Lewis.

In mid-January, Peter and Edna departed for West Palm Springs, Florida. Peter returned in March telling an ever-interested press that his wife had decided to stay a couple of weeks longer. While he didn't say she wasn't feeling well, often when they traveled he returned before she did, and illness was given as the reason. Edna didn't linger long, however, as later the same month she and Peter left to spend a few days in New Orleans. Edna returned to Lewis, hosted several gatherings in May, then left in June to spend the summer with Minnie in Idaho.

Peter, at about this time, stopped at the office of the News Telegraph to voice an opinion on a just-enacted tax increase. He railed *"particularly in regard to the capital extension matter, which he branded as an outrage."* A paper of conservative political views, the Telegraph used Hopley's statement in a front-page article.

Peter Hopley, early in life, considered himself a Democrat. He was, however, a conservative and decidedly Capitalistic sort of Democrat. Either the party evolved or Peter did, and he left, according to a Telegraph interview, to become an independent voter who leaned Republican.

He made the news days later when he hired two men to finish tearing down the *"old Hopley feed and stallion barn."*

1913 would not have been a typical Hopley year had it not included an embarrassing accident (which will be detailed later), a horse-buying trip to Europe (he left shortly after Edna went to Idaho), and a lawsuit. This one, filed a few days before Thanksgiving, named a few of Edna's relatives. Peter and Harry had, some years earlier, acquired the 80 acres Edna's father was buying when he was found dead near Turkey Creek in 1860. This must have been a tangled estate. Joe Everly died young (39) and unexpectedly, not having time to make preparations for the event. He owed money on the land and may have had other debts. He had a second wife and five children, all from his first marriage.

While the details are unclear, it appears that sixty-three years after Joe Everly met his fate, twenty years after Peter and Harry bought the land, some heirs of Everly claimed at least partial rights of ownership. Hopley, as plaintiff, filed a petition stating the land (in section 26 of Washington Township) was clearly owned by him and his son, Harry. Numerous names were listed, some Everly and some named Watson, and the petition challenged them to come forward and defend any claim they were alleged to have, or forever hold their peace.

(We find it curious that members of the Watson family were listed, as evidence was offered that one Jacob Watson was most likely the person who thumped the drunken Everly on the skull, resulting in his death. Perhaps these were from a different Watson family, but the Jacob

Watsons and Joseph Everlys were neighbors and Watson may have loaned Everly money.

While the violent death of Joe Everly may or may not have been a part of this one, petitions of this type were common at the time. Some Iowa land was settled before surveys were complete. Original surveys were not always precisely accurate. The location of river beds changed. These suits were often not contested, were entered into as a legal means of establishing a clear title that would not later be questioned.

# Chapter Seven

In 1914 a war would begin in Europe—a war that impacted the family long after an armistice was signed. Peter Hopley made his last trip across the Atlantic in 1914. He also acquired an automobile. Peter, content for years to travel by train and horse-drawn conveyance, chose an Aero. His wife opted for a Studebaker. Edna retained a Lewis resident named Harry Allyn to be her chauffeur *"for the summer season."*

Harry Hopley, then thirty-three and the "Son" in "Hopley and Son," followed his father's lead and made a call at the newspaper office himself. He thought the Telegraph editor would be interested in his estimation of the impact the war was, and would continue to have, on the Hopley horse trade. He brought with him a letter recently received from a French breeder the Hopleys had done business with. The war, although it had just begun, had already decimated the horse population. French and English military, in what amounted to pointless slaughter, sent waves of cavalry into German machine gun fire, barbed wire and artillery. Horses were confiscated by the government and pressed into service to pull heavy guns, ambulances, haul supplies. It would take, Harry was quoted as saying, *"at least twenty years for the horse business to recover."* Hogs, he said, would replace horses on the Hopley farms, at least for a few years. About 1500 swine were on the farm then, he noted, and more soon would be.

Harry was in the news again that summer when, while driving his new Overland Roadster to Omaha to pick up his wife, he was involved in a collision. The westbound Overland met an eastbound horse and buggy. Behind the buggy was a Ford and a driver anxious to pass. He did so at the crest of a hill. There were no serious injuries, but the Ford was *"rendered ready for the junk heap."*

Edna Hopley, in 1914, observed her fifty-eighth birthday. She was experiencing increasing issues with her health.

The problem was not new. In 1888 she gave birth to her eighth child, a daughter named Gertrude. A year later, suffering from membranous croup, the baby died. Then, in mid-July, 1895, another child was lost. The oldest, Beulah, had recently turned twenty. Of her the Lewis Standard wrote: *She was an exceptionally bright young woman, highly respected and esteemed among a circle of friends and acquaintances that is perhaps larger than that enjoyed by any other young woman in the county.*

A student, she was home for the summer, spending time with her mother in the garden, enjoying herself with friends and high school classmates. She was ten years old when the family moved into the newly-built house on Oregon Street. Her memory of life as it had been in the simple dwelling on the farm gave her an appreciation of the elegant home her younger siblings could not have had.

She arose early on the morning of Tuesday, July 16 and, as she had been doing for years, helped Edna fix breakfast. Peter enjoyed having the morning meal with his children, and he wanted it early. It was his custom to be on the farm while chores were being done, to get progress reports from his foreman, to see the hired men off to the field.

Seated at the table that morning was Margaret, then eighteen and looking forward to college in the fall. Edith (Eda) was sixteen; Harry, fourteen; Edna, twelve; Minnie and Mary were nine. Little Wayland was but a year old and may have slept in.

Breakfast had just been completed when, at about 7:30, Beulah went into convulsions. Newspaper articles from previous years tell of Edna taking Beulah to Arizona and elsewhere *"for her health,"* but do not tell us whether she suffered from epilepsy or a similar condition. She lost consciousness and was dead within hours.

Reports of Edna's health problems began to make the news soon thereafter. These were initially one or two-line items, buried in the social column—"*Mrs. Peter Hopley, who has been unwell, has gone to Colfax for the mineral spa.*" Years passed, and by 1914 her life had become one of cycles. There were balls and parties, invitations received and extended, shopping trips and entertainment (when Peter later wrote that he had given most of his income and a large portion of his wealth to their children because neither he nor his wife needed much, he was exercising a selective memory). Edna's social agenda was interrupted by periodic and often extended illness.

A typical item appeared in the Lewis Standard in April of 1899, when Edna was forty-three years old: "*Mrs. Peter Hopley recently returned home after spending several weeks in Florida, where she went for her health.*"

She sought various treatments, including that recommended by William's son-in-law, Dr. C.L. Campbell of Atlantic.

The year was 1906. That spring, with Harry overseeing the farms, Peter and Edna, along with daughter Eda, took an extended trip abroad. With Peter sometimes accompanying them, other times off in search of horses, the women toured England and visited relatives and friends made on previous trips. In late August, three months after arriving, they boarded a steamer bound for New York.

While still in the English Channel, several passengers and crew members observed what was described as an "enormous sea serpent." After a few moments the creature submerged and was seen no more. News of the incident was treated much as a UFO sighting might be today—the sort of below-the-fold article readers like to talk about in coffee shops. A report was telegraphed to the U.S. Among those listed in New York newspapers as having seen the monster was Peter Hopley of Lewis, Iowa. The article was picked up by Cass County papers while the Hopleys were still at sea. Reporters from Lewis and Atlantic had something other than the routine questions that followed a typical Peter Hopley return.

No mention was made as to whether either Edna or Eda saw the "sea serpent." Mother and daughter remained in New York for a few days. Either upon return or shortly thereafter Edna's "stomach problems" returned. Before the end of September she was in the Mayo Clinic, taken there personally by Dr. Campbell.

Whatever was done at Mayo provided no lasting effect. Edna returned home, reportedly better, resumed her active life. She was ill again in a few months.

In 1907 newspapers reported that Peter was on his way home from Europe with *"more horses. Mrs. Hopley is not feeling well, and her friends are having some anxiety."*

At times Peter hired a private nurse who would take a room in the mansion and give his wife around-the-clock attention. Other times the daughters took turns staying with her.

She made increasingly frequent trips to Colfax. In that central Iowa town, in 1875, miners seeking coal discovered an underground reservoir of water having an exceptionally high mineral content. Town officials and entrepreneurs seized the opportunity. The town was advertised as being a Mecca for people plagued by various maladies. Appropriate facilities, some quite luxurious, were opened to the public. According to a city history there were, at one time, nine hotels offering mineral baths and spas. Four bottling companies dispensed the elixir, selling wholesale to drug stores and by direct mail order to consumers.

The Lewis Standard, between the mid-1890s and the time of Edna's death in 1919, make frequent reference to the Colfax connection. These were almost always a single sentence, with minimal elaboration or speculation.

*Mrs. Peter Hopley left today for Colfax, where she will receive treatments.*

Two years later, this:

*Mr. Peter Hopley returned today from Colfax, where he visited his wife.*

She returned home shortly thereafter, but not for long.

*Mrs. Peter Hopley arrived on the Rock Island from Colfax, and is reportedly much improved.*

Exactly what caused these recurring periods of illness is unknown. References are made to a "stomach problem." When she collapsed and died the corresponding news article said she had suffered for years from "high blood pressure." On other occasions she reportedly had pneumonia.

There were whispers, however, that at least some of Mrs. Hopley "spells" resulted from the excessive consumption of a certain substance.

She lived in a time when rumors of this nature were common, and there were plenty of old-timers who remembered her father, and how and why he was killed. The anti-alcohol faction, during Edna Hopley's lifetime, reached their pinnacle of power and influence. They zealously pursued a constitutional amendment mandating a nation-wide prohibition on manufacture, sale, and consumption. While they achieved this goal the year after Edna died, they'd started decades earlier. As early as the 1870s the anti-saloon movement in Iowa was successful in electing politicians who enacted a series of regulatory statutes controlling alcohol. Most voters agreed that a certain level of control was necessary. So called "tee-totalers," as dedicated to their cause as abolitionists had been to theirs, wanted the extreme, would settle only for total abstinence, and felt strict laws were the only way to get there.

State laws enabled cities and counties to be more restrictive, which many were. Federal prohibition, when it came, had limited impact on Iowans, as they had years of experience in circumventing whatever regulations were passed.

There was a sharp division between "wet" and "dry" factions, with little refuge in the center. Towns as small as Lewis were as subject to polarization as any. Lewis churches favored prohibition. The most dedicated workers toward this goal tended to be devout women of the church. Most of them were not a part of the elite social circle that Edna Hopley belonged to.

The relationship Peter and Edna Hopley had with the church does not appear to be as strong as was that of Peter's parents. His father, the abolitionist, was close to the Congregational Church's abolitionist minister, Reverend Hitchcock. He and his wife and children joined that church. The family, including young Peter, were said to have attended regularly. Later, when he went west, he fell out of the habit. When he returned and married he belonged, his children were baptized. Peter almost certainly attended at times—Easter was good, as was Christmas.

Certainly his wife and children, at least while the family was young, were regulars, but he traveled and his work was his priority. His lifetime relationship with the church, even in his old age, is indicative of someone who belonged because it was socially expected, couldn't hurt business, and one never knew when one might need a preacher.

Edna once took him to a Chautauqua at which Billy Sunday preached. The evangelist's standard Chautauqua fare had him dashing down the aisle and "sliding into home for Jesus." His message included reference to sin as his mortal foe. *"As long as I have a fist, I'll hit it. As long as I have a foot I'll kick it. As long as I have a tooth I'll bite it. And when I'm old and fist-less and foot-less and tooth-less. . ."* and so on.

Peter was probably not impressed. Most likely he went either to see if Billy Sunday was as bizarre as he'd been told, or because Edna insisted.

We find references to organizations that he and his wife belonged to and actively supported. Peter was a practicing Mason and became an officer in the Shrine. He belonged to various livestock and agricultural organizations. The church is mentioned, but this membership appears to have been more passive than was the case with other affiliations.

Peter, in writing of his success, credits hard work, his wife, ambition, nerve, and sound decisions. Many men of his day, perhaps even most of them, would have given some credit to God. The nearest he comes, in his writings that remain, is to say that man must have *"faith in Mother Nature."* We do not know if the decision to capitalize the first letter of those two words was his, or that of an editor.

Peter was less than a devoted supporter of the church. He quite likely played cards for money, probably for big money. Whether Peter imbibed while playing poker we don't know. Others certainly did. It seems safe to assume that at some of the fine dinners he and Edna participated in a bit of wine was served. The same was true of parties they attended. When gentlemen retired to the smoking room for a cigar they quite likely, even though it may not have been exactly legal, enjoyed a glass of brandy or fine bourbon. Prohibitionists did not approve.

From small happenings, whether innocent or not, particularly in a town small enough for everyone to know everyone, rumors can spread and grow. Exaggerations are made. Edna may have never touched a drop. I think it unlikely that she did so to excess, or that she went to Colfax to dry out. Undeniable, however, is the fact that her father had a drinking problem, and she had opportunity, wealth, and leisure. The Hopley fortune was wasted by descendants with a weakness for gambling and drink. Those flaws can be connected to their predecessors.

Peter and Edna's grandsons expanded, developing vices of their own.

# Chapter Eight

As the house in Lewis was being completed the Hopley family, perhaps for a couple of years, lived in town during the winter, on the farm in the summer. This did not last long. Edna had a taste of city life, of the social status available to her, and settled in. Her husband became a commuter. Often by horseback, other times in a wagon or buggy drawn by a fine gaited horse, he went about his business—in style. J.B. Enton was publisher of the Lewis Independent, and in June of 1884 Peter gave him a ride.

*Peter Hopley is the owner of a Boss Road Cart he imported from Chicago. The other day he hitched his two-minute bay to it and took this writer in. It is so deep and wide and immense that it reminds us of the old Pennsylvania style of wagon architecture. We expected to be dumped out at the first street crossing, but instead she rode the waves with the grace of an ocean steamer, with the same undulating motion as that imparted by a vessel on the waves. As Peter says, "By G-d, she's a Joe dandy."*

The "Boss Road Cart" was a lightweight, snappy-looking four-wheeled horse-drawn vehicle with leaf-spring suspension. Carriages of this type were later equipped with gasoline engines and the car was born. Enton's reference to a "two-minute bay" had to do with the horse's speed. Top-quality, gaited harness horses of the day could trot the mile in 2½ minutes, more or less. Animals in that class—those that could pull a buggy a mile in less than three minutes—were sometimes called "two-minute" bays or chestnuts or whatever their color.

The roads Peter Hopley traveled to the farm were narrow and, in wet weather, a bog. His farm was on the east side of the river and to get there he need only cross Turkey Creek. Harry's place was on the west side of the East Nishnabotna, through flat bottom land prone to flooding. In the 1920s, when the river was straightened, the old "bottom road" was intersected by drainage ditches; trenches designed to move water to the river. Across these ditches simple plank bridges were erected. They had no railings.

Forty years after Peter died his youngest son, who was inclined to drive faster than he should have, knocked some manure from his boots (or maybe not), climbed into his Cadillac for a trip to town. He almost always drove with the stub of a burned-out cigar clenched in the corner of his mouth. Hickory Hopley, who had a broken leg and limited mobility because of the cast, stretched out in the back seat.

The road was still dirt and little-used. For Hopley it was, as it had been for his father, a short-cut to Lewis. A better route, but a couple of miles longer, was east to the highway, then south.

Wayland Hopley knew it had rained hard two or three nights earlier. The road had dried, though, and he chose it. He did not know one of the plank bridges had washed out. His Cadillac was the first vehicle to travel the road since the storm. Other than in an ambulance, the trip would be Wayland Hopley Sr.'s last.

John, fifteen years older than Peter, came to America, returned to England, finally coming to this country to stay in 1859. He farmed with his father before buying a place of his own north and east of Lewis. In 1872 he co-signed the note with which Peter bought his first farm. Shortly thereafter, John moved on to Colorado in the quest for gold (although there is some disagreement on this. Some say John went west to farm). His widowed mother lived with him there, but only for a short time. John found no gold, or didn't do well with the farm, returned to the Lewis area and built a house on what was called the "county farm road." His mother, known locally as "Grandma Hopley," made her home in town until her death. (She lived in a small house on the north side of Main Street 1 ½ blocks west of where the water tower now is.)

"Grandma" Francis Hopley, who outlived her husband by three decades, became somewhat of a local character and a regular at the annual Old Settlers Reunion. In August of 1900, in her 94th year and unable to walk, she was helped onto center stage at the Crystal Lake pavilion and was recognized by a crowd estimated to number ten thousand (probably an exaggeration). Peter and Edna and family were in attendance, and Peter shared some often-told stories of his youth in the area.

Throughout the afternoon well-wishers stopped by the picnic table where "Grandpa" Hopley was seated and listened as she told, with a pleasant British accent, of how she and her family encountered a storm while crossing the Atlantic (it would be interesting to know which version of the crossing she told) and of her family's early days in Cass County. The Atlantic Daily Telegraph article went on to report that, although she had some physical impairments, *"she is still hale and hearty. Her eyesight is so good she reads ordinary print with ease, and has no need of spectacles."*

While he was not a central figure, having been dead two years, John Hopley was prominently referred to in a complex series of legal actions that resulted from business dealings in Lewis. Isaac Dickerson (for whom Lewis's Dickerson Addition is named) was, in the view of some, a bit of a shyster. There existed adequate reasons for people to feel this way.

Dickerson, born in Pennsylvania in 1830, came to Iowa with his family at the age of fourteen. He grew up in the Oskaloosa area, married in 1853, moved two or three times before he and his young family settled n Lewis in 1856, at about the same time as the Hopleys. Isaac and Olivia had six children, three sons and three daughters. According to Lafe Young's 1877 county history, Isaac opened a dry goods store in Lewis. He also became Lewis postmaster, holding this position from 1856-61. Young credits Dickerson with the introduction of "boxes" or "pigeon holes," to the post office, and, Young writes, *the event was one of importance to the villagers."* Dickerson left the post office upon being elected country treasurer, which at the time was the combined office of treasurer and recorder. He bought land not to farm but to hold for speculation.

As a county official he had access to affairs that others did not. Everyone knew the railroad was coming. Having knowledge of where offered a golden opportunity. If Dickerson took advantage of what he knew, he wasn't the only one. He was among the founders of the "Atlantic Township Company," invested in a manner that may not have been entirely ethical, and profited. His "Atlantic Township Company" sold lots and worked with the railroad in forming and laying out the town. Dickerson left Lewis to build an elegant home in the new city—a city that would soon take the seat of county government from his former hometown. He served several terms of mayor in Atlantic, one or two as councilman. Atlantic might have honored him as a founding father had it not been for the bank incident.

Dickerson teamed with a brother, A.W. Dickerson (born the year after Isaac), to open a real estate office. Together they bought and sold considerable property, some on commission, some for themselves. To prospective buyers who lacked the cash and were either unwilling or unable to acquire a conventional loan, the Dickersons offered terms. Their loans were at high interest, foreclosures undoubtedly took place. In 1870 Isaac was the motivating force behind the founding of the Cass County Bank in Lewis. His brother was a partner and cashier. An article in the Lewis paper refers to a son as being an employee. In 1876 the bank was sold (with Dickerson retaining an undisclosed but apparently sizeable portion) and reorganized as a state bank. J.C. Yetzer was named president, Isaac Dickerson, Vice President, and A.W. Dickerson was Assistant Cashier.

The bank, by outward appearances, did well until there came a financial downturn called the "panic of 1893." A number of banks around the country failed, trust in these institutions diminished, and a few investors sought to get their money out of Dickerson's. They didn't get much. The bank closed and went into receivership. Among those named to oversight was Peter Hopley. An auditor was retained, a number of discrepancies and questionable loans revealed, including some made to members of the board of directors. There were allegations that what had been going on was not just incompetent banking; it was criminal. A grand jury convened, evidence was considered, indictments were issued.

Trial opened in 1895, with a most impressive cast of lawyers representing each side. The noted Smith McPherson of Red Oak, whose career included a stint on the Iowa Supreme Court, assisted with the prosecution. Dickerson's side hired a number of defense lawyers, including Clyde Genung. Genung was as good at his job as any to be found, and was much in demand. He was among the lawyers who secured the acquittal of Reverend George Kelley after the minister confessed to the 1912 Villisca ax murders.

The Dickerson trial had all the elements of a pot-boiler. Virtually everyone in the county knew Isaac Dickerson. For nearly forty years he'd been in the public eye; postmaster, elected county and city official, developer, realtor, a man some might have called a loan shark, and during the 1880s and early 90s newspaper ads for his real estate listings were standard front-page fare. The trial would test banking laws intended to protect depositors and stabilize banks. Lawyers handling the case had talent and material and were capable of sterling performances. Lewis area residents, many of which either had a financial stake or knew someone who did, were keenly interested. The presiding judge agreed that feelings ran so high a fair trial could not be had in Cass County, and moved the proceedings to Mills County. Local newspapers followed every twist and turn; the Telegraph even retained a special reporter who was present during the entire trial, posting daily accounts.

The Telegraph's correspondent spent several weekends in Glenwood, enabling him to do articles on details, such as how jurors and participants on both sides spent their days off. He noted that if those who went to church did so with the same regularity at home they demonstrated during the trial, local ministers would be amazed and gratified.

The trial would probably have been talked about for years had it not been so lengthy—it went on for weeks—and so tedious. The state's star witness was an accountant. He was called and recalled, then called and recalled again. Every line, every total, was subject to the most minute scrutiny. Clyde Genung was a master at turning a relatively simple issue into a complex one. Delay followed recess followed conference followed further delay.

A witness would be asked a technical question about a particular technique of accounting. After a lengthy answer, interrupted by constant objections, cross-examination, also subject to repeated objections, would begin. This continued, day after day, week after week, until even reporters grew weary of it all. When the criminal trial finally ended the verdict did not satisfy many of those who had lost money when the bank failed, although guilty verdicts were found. Yetzer and A.W. Dickerson went to jail. Sixty-five year old Isaac, who some thought at least as culpable, did not. He closed his office, sold his house, took his money and moved to Missouri. At the time of his death in 1911, the Telegraph wrote that Dickerson *"left Atlantic under a cloud following the failure of the Cass County Bank. J.C. Yetzer and A.W. Dickerson were found guilty and sent to the penitentiary. Isaac Dickerson escaped incarceration."*

Civil suits, most of which had been pending during the criminal trial, began. The case would drag on for another five years. One of actions involved John Hopley, and drew his brothers Peter and William into a sticky situation.

John, in the mid to late 1880s, was on the verge of trouble—personal, financial, and physical. One problem had to do with a loan of $2000 from Dickerson's Cass County Bank of Lewis. John applied, but apparently needed a co-signer. Twenty years earlier he had co-signed a note with which Peter bought his first farm. Peter returned the favor.

John probably needed the money to pay medical expenses. On the other hand, it may have gone to the ponies. There's also a possibility the money went to an ex-wife. Whatever, he later returned to the bank and allegedly stole the original copy of the note. If true, and subsequent testimony leaves little doubt, this left the bank without proof of the loan.

In the fall of 1893, before the bank went under, John's health took a turn for the worse. He wanted to go to Battle Creek, Michigan, to seek treatment. He did not, however, have the funds. He was in need of $75. Testimony was offered that A.W. Dickerson (the bank's cashier) hearing of John's plight, sent a messenger with $75 and word that the money was a gift to help cover the expense of treatment. John reportedly was deeply touched, said he had badly misjudged Dickerson. He repented, felt suddenly so wretched about his misdeed with the note that he signed an otherwise blank piece of paper, a hand-made form of a promissory contract, and sent the messenger back to Dickerson telling him to fill in the amount he, John Hopley, owed. Dickerson did. John then boarded a train, with his brother William accompanying him, and set off for Battle Creek and another round at his favorite sanatorium. He got as far as Valpariso, Indiana, and died.

Was the note valid? That the signature was John's was not contested. Dickerson readily acknowledged that he'd filled in the amount based on the previous, now missing, note. He did not include the $75. The question was whether or not John, a very sick man, signing his name to a blank piece of paper, was lawfully executing a promissory note.

An argument was made that the note was not binding. All John did was sign a paper. The amount was added by Dickerson. This, it was contended, was out of order. John's signature should have been attached only after the amount of obligation was reduced to writing. His intent, it was argued, may have been no more than a "thank you." Testimony that he sent word for Dickerson to fill in an amount was challenged. Only John knew what was in his mind, and John was dead.

Peter Hopley, co-signer and liable if the judge ruled for Dickerson, said nothing for public consumption. He probably preferred to not be asked why the brother of one of the wealthiest men in the county had to seek charity to pay medical expenses.

Regardless, the judge ruled the note was legitimate.

There may have been perfectly good reasons why Peter's relationship with big brother John was a bit strained. John had his issues, one of which was women. His first wife was left in Colorado; presumably following a legitimate divorce. The second died young, and under unusual circumstances. Her name was Gertrude (not to be confused with Peter and Edna's daughter, Gertrude). She and John, along with their son and daughter, lived on a farm about five miles south of Atlantic (where the county home was later located). In February of 1879 a news article tells us four people—Mrs. Hopley, her son, along with a hired man and hired girl, all became ill due to "being poisoned." John is not mentioned, so we assume he was either not home or had not ingested whatever made the others ill. His wife was the worst of the lot, there being some concern that she might not recover. The Telegraph article speculates that the water well might have been poisoned and asks what kind of human being would do such a thing?

John and Gertrude divorced shortly thereafter. Then, in July of 1881, she died of "quick consumption," having been in poor health since the poisoning. Even though divorced, John took charge. Gertrude's funeral was held in his home. The article that appeared in the Daily Telegraph at the time of her death concludes by informing readers that Gertrude's *"married life was quite unhappy and a short time ago she secured a divorce from her husband. Death was undoubtedly welcomed as a kindly messenger."*

She was 39 years old.

Four years later John married Blanche Seamans, a Cass County girl and divorcee then twenty-four years of age. He was fifty-one. Their troubles started shortly following the wedding.

Two years after saying "I do," Blanche let her regrets be known. Divorce was not as common in the 1880s as it later became. A man with John's marital history being sued by his third wife, she already once-divorced, on the grounds of "cruel and inhumane treatment" made the news. This story provided the sort of sensational reading subscribers relished, and was worthy of the front page.

Blanche not only wanted out, she felt mistreated to the extent she asked for a $10,000 settlement. This was a lot of money, particularly considering John's financial situation, which was rather anemic. In September a judge ruled that John was to pay Blanche $25 per month, plus $100 attorney fees, until such time as a final decree was issued. Both sides were given the opportunity to prepare their cases.

By November, Blanche had changed her mind. She and John reconciled. Her bliss was fleeting, however, and a few months later she changed course once again and reinstituted divorce proceedings. Whatever the nature of John's cruel treatment, she would tolerate no more. By 1889 they were permanently divorced and, in July of that year, Blanche filed another suit. This one alleged slander. A part of John's mistreatment was saying very bad things about her, or so she claimed. Slander suits are difficult. Proving a person said damaging things is not sufficient. Even if the statements were untrue, and can be demonstrated to be false, plaintiff must also show that defendant knew the statements were untrue at the time they were uttered. Defendant, in this case John, could say that when he said what he said he had reason to believe the veracity. And if certain uncomplimentary things were said about the defendant's wife, who knew her better than he? Whether her suit had merit or not, Blanche did not get to trial.

Not everyone disliked John Hopley. Early in 1890, with Lafe Young, founder of the Atlantic Telegraph delivering the keynote speech, a group of friends hosted a banquet in John's honor. The event was held at the Park Hotel. Lafe, a politician and orator of note, delivered a rousing address depicting what a fine fellow Mr. Hopley was. The article says a sumptuous meal was served. Details of the delicacies were not given, but a paid ad in the same edition gives a sampling of what the Park Hotel kitchen had to offer:

*"A first course of select oysters, New York Count variety, is followed by a relish tray with radishes, celery, and assorted nuts. Salad was next, then boiled trout with wine sauce. Roast beef au jus was one of the entrée choices, as was roast goose with oyster dressing, roast chicken with sage dressing, and baked quail with pan sauce served on toast. Dessert was mince pie, lemon pie,"* and on and on and on. Diners at the Park Hotel, as was the case at the Whitney and the Pullman, were well taken care of.

No specific reason for the banquet was given in the Telegraph article. There was no sale to celebrate, no noteworthy event in John's life, at least none mentioned, that brought about the honor. One of the guests, perhaps the organizer, was Alf Bailey of Grant. Bailey had, like John Hopley, been born in England, and the two were close.

It may have been that because Hopley was a sick man there were some who knew him and wanted a festive occasion while he was there to enjoy it.

We are not told the specifics of his ailment. Tuberculosis is a possibility. ("Quick consumption," listed as the cause of his second wife's death, was a term often used for tuberculosis. We find no record, though, of Gertrude being sent anywhere for treatments.) Whatever the condition, John seems to have benefitted from visits to a Michigan sanatorium. He went there often, sometimes twice a year. Upon return he was known to call on the newspaper office and literally gush with enthusiasm. The sanatorium offered miracles, in his view, and he wanted others to know.

He also went to a lot of horse races. Harness racing, in the 1880s and 90s, was an immensely popular sport. Probably all the Hopley brothers, given their relationship with equines, enjoyed a good contest. Considering the indications we have that some of them may have gambled more than just a little, it would not be surprising if Peter and William made a few trips to the pari-mutuel window.

None, though, were involved to the extent of John. He invested, if such is the right word—or at least so he claimed. An 1891 Telegraph article reports that he went to a harness horse sale in Chicago and bought two supposedly fine stallions—"Spaulding" and "Bonnie Wilkes." Although the latter was from the noted "Wilkes" bloodline, records available at the National Harness Horse Museum and Hall of Fame, located in Goshen, New York, indicate neither Spaulding nor Bonnie Wilkes amounted to much. (Bonnie Wilkes, according to their records, was a mare instead of a stallion.) In October of the same year he *"bought one of Jack Colwell's fine racing colts. The consideration was $250."*

A news article tells us John was going to stable his newly-acquired horses at his *"trotting horse farm in northern Iowa."* A later item reported that a horse barn he was building near Fonda was nearly completed.

That John lived in Cass County, had farmland here, but was keeping "his" trotting horses in northern Iowa tells us there may have been a partner; or perhaps several. This would not have been unusual. John might have gotten a "fine racing colt" from jack Colwell for $250, but it's doubtful much at the Chicago auction went for that price. Top-quality trotting horses could demand $100,000 and more. Owning one was risky. A misstep, a broken leg, illness, a collision on the track, and a huge investment was worth no more than dog food. Conglomerates often owned the good and potentially good ones, spreading the risk, and such is still the case today.

Another race horse John told the papers he had a part of was named "Iowa Chief," probably the best of those John claimed as his. This horse ran a major race in Phoenix in January of 1893. He took three heats out of five, with a best time of 2:35.

Races of that era were run in heats because endurance was as important as speed. A buggy horse that went a mile and needed a breather was not ideal. To make races a test of stamina rules required that a horse win three heats, each a mile long. Horses trotted a mile, lined up and did it again, and kept at it until one had taken three. Some of those races lasted a long time. In buying a horse, or studying bloodlines, discriminating purchasers wanted to know how fast the horse was in the 2nd, 3rd, and subsequent heats. Iowa Chief was the type they were looking for. He was running strong after five miles, was a horse that could take a buggy from Lewis to Atlantic in twenty minutes. Iowa Chief was fast and, had things not worked out the way they did, might have made John a good deal of money.

On the other hand, much of the story of John's horse investments may have been a sham. A librarian at the National Harness Racing museum was kind enough to check the registration and racing records of all horses John told newspapers he owned. Hopley's name does not appear, there's no record of Spaulding ever running in a sanctioned race and, while Iowa Chief was owned at different times by different investors, John Hopley is not listed as one of them. This does not mean John was untruthful—he may have been a silent partner or the records incomplete or incorrect. Given, however, other things we know about John's life and character there is reason to wonder.

John had sources of income. We see periodic notices that he had cattle on feed, shipped loads to market—usually Colorado. But he also had horses, and if he owned a part of animals like Iowa Chief the cost was high. Betting on them, particularly the slow ones, could be expensive as well, although we don't know how John did in that regard.

The "panic of 1893" was nearly as bad for horse racing speculators as it was banking. Investors with discretionary cash to buy part-interest in trotters looked for the exit. There were few who wanted in. High-risk investors like John Hopley, if that's indeed what he was, took a bath. A stallion worth a fortune a year earlier might bring half that, or less. Races continued. Fast animals were still fast, fans remained loyal, betting lines were intact, but the incentive to hazard large amounts of capital declined. By the time it returned, there were Overland Roadsters.

Like that of many other Hopleys, when John passed his estate was a long time in settling. There were too many debts, too many notes; some consigned to William, some to Peter. Even Etta, John's only daughter, got into the act. Etta was 13 when her mother became desperately ill, allegedly from poison. She was 14 when her parents divorced after an "unhappy marriage," and 15 when her mother died. She probably was not on the best of terms with John.

With John dead, she sued William. Plaintiffs were lumped together—the biggest was the Cass County bank, which held notes signed by John totaling about $11,000. His assets did not approach that amount. The case was finally brought before a jury in 1897, four years after John died. The verdict was for the plaintiff in the amount of $15,000.

Back in 1893, with John unwell and slipping, asking for money with which to receive treatments, Peter and William may have harbored the feeling that keeping John alive was an expensive proposition in more ways than one.

Like John, Joseph (1850-1903), did not share his brother's success, at least from a financial standpoint. Peter's youngest sibling went west, maybe to farm, maybe to chase gold, but spent only a short time in Colorado. He also returned, poorer but perhaps wiser, to Lewis. His occupation was recorded, at various times, as "livestock dealer" and "farmer." He was forty years old when he married Hattie Baker, who had just turned twenty-one. Joseph rarely rated mention in the papers, in part because he relocated several times; Lee County, Cass County, Colorado, back to Butler County in Iowa, and then once again to the Atlantic area, and when he did the news was not necessarily positive.

Joseph was but fifty-three years of age when died in 1903. The managing editor of the Lewis Standard, Charles Willey, cultivated his relationship with the Okells, the Hopleys, the Montagues, the Woodwards, the Kennedys and the Harris family. He relied on people named Zike and Delean and Wissler and Albright and Marker and

Burkhalter and Ebert and Ward and Meredith for news items of both substance and social interest. When a member of those families died his coverage was typically rife with superlatives. Depictions ran the gamut from "sturdy pioneers," "among the most respected in the area," "most popular and well-liked young lady in the county," "an irreplaceable loss," "throngs of mourners," and so on. What he wrote when Joseph Hopley passed is markedly lacking in these tributes, therefore a bit out-of-character for a leading family obit. We reprint it as it appeared in his paper on November 19, 1903.

*Joseph Hopley died in Chicago Friday, whither he had gone about six weeks previous for medical treatment. An operation was performed, which was the immediate cause of his decease.*

*Mr. Hopley had been ailing for some years, and gradually grew worse. His ailment was an intestinal affection, and there seemed to be no cure for it. As a last resort, with the hope of prolonging life for a short time, the knife was resorted to, and with the usual result life came to a sudden termination.*

*Deceased was born in England in 1850. At an early age he came with his parents to this country and settled in Lee County, this state. After remaining there a short time he came with the rest of the family to Cass County, which has since been his home except for a short time spent in Colorado. He was united in marriage to Hattie Baker on July 4, 1889. A loving wife and five children remain to mourn his loss.*

*Funeral services were held at the Odd Fellows' Hall, Atlantic, Monday, November 16th, at 10 o'clock a.m., conducted in accordance with the ritual of the order, of which he was a worthy member. The remains were taken to Oakwood cemetery for interment.*

Willey offers a bland and incomplete sketch. No mention is made regarding what Joseph did for a living. The only affiliation cited is that he was a member of the Odd Fellows. Information having to do with achievements, other than having five children (none of which have their names mentioned) is absent. Joseph owned some land when he died, having farmed near the "Poor Farm" south of Atlantic. His estate was modest, with much of his monetary worth consumed during his lengthy illness.

Willey's low regard for surgery—"*the knife was resorted to, and with the usual result life came to a sudden termination*"—must have been on his mind when he wrote his final article some thirty years later. By that time he was himself plagued by health issues, one of which was advanced cataracts. He was losing his eyesight. The only chance to save his vision was to undergo what was then a high-risk procedure. Willey, his paper losing money in the Depression, fearing that surgery would not succeed, sold the Standard to the Griswold American. Two years later, blind, living alone in the cluttered building that once housed his newspaper, his condition worsened. He was hospitalized for a few weeks in Atlantic, then passed away.

# Chapter Nine

William Hopley, according to his obituary, was seventeen when, as a runaway, he left England. This was presumably not to his father's liking, in part because the boy was considered indentured, but any ill feelings were temporary. William returned to England to fetch his siblings while his father was said to be deeply involved in anti-slavery activities in Lee County. William and his parents reunited there, then in 1856 moved to Cass County. William partnered with his father for a year or two on a dairy farm, after which he bought land of his own. By the time Peter went west William had a sizeable number of acres, the dairy farm giving way to beef cattle, hogs, sheep and crops.

His father, Thomas, agreed with Lincoln and northern Republicans on the slavery issue, feeling the practice could not be tolerated anywhere. War, with Lincoln's election, was inevitable. Thousands of young men from Iowa answered the call.

William Hopley was not among them. In 1862, a year after the war began, Governor Kirkwood instituted measures to place hundreds of thousands of additional Iowans in the Union army. Still, William Hopley, twenty-five and single, stayed home. John Hopley was twenty-nine when Fort Sumpter was fired upon. James was twenty, Thomas Jr. was twenty-eight. We find no record that any of them served.

*(The Hopley boys might be compared to George Madden, another young man who settled in Southwest Iowa in at about the time the Hopley family arrived. Life was a struggle, but*

*he and his wife had paid for their farm and might have become prosperous had he not died in the Civil War. In the years prior, Madden kept a daily journal. He was an astute observer of people, subscribed to newspapers, and kept well informed on current events. Unlike Thomas Hopley, he was not a Lincoln supporter. He was not an abolitionist. He had an insider's view of how national turbulence, slavery issues, and an approaching war impacted southwest Iowans. In 1862, as thirty-three year old Madden made arrangements for his wife to live with his parents, for someone to farm his land, he wrote these lines:*

*"Now is the trying time. Let every Union man stand shoulder to shoulder regardless of party in defense of the constitution. But I am sorry to say there are some few individuals who are devising every means to evade the draft, who have, heretofore, been very loud in favor of the war and wanted everybody else but themselves to go and everyone was a traitor who did not suit their views in politics.*

*Practice is far above profession in my estimation and any man can be a brave man where there is no danger. We all have our views. We cannot agree with the administration in every particular, especially in party politics, but nevertheless it is our duty to stand by our government as long as the President stands by the constitution.)*

Madden, in writing about Iowans who had a stance but evaded wartime service, had families such as the Hopleys in mind. Peter, at fourteen, was too young; as was Joseph. Why his other brothers, sons of a man who felt as strongly as Thomas Hopley did about the central issue of the war, stayed out is a question that cannot now be answered. It may be that, while Thomas opposed slavery, he was not committed to the preservation of the Union. He had grown to adulthood in England. Although England remained neutral, there were fears in the north as the war progressed that she might, in part because of cotton, side with the Confederacy. It is also possible that Thomas was not as active in the cause as he was reported, after his death, to have been.

Regardless, the sons of Thomas Hopley did not interrupt their lives for a war. Their sons and grandsons, however, did. Few Cass County families lost to the extent the Hopleys did during World War II—losses that contributed to the end of an era.

In February of 1864 William married Mary Okell, returning to Lee County to do so (while Mary had relatives in Lewis, it's not clear whether she was living there or in Lee County prior to the marriage.) Just over a year later, on the day of Lincoln's assassination, the young couple was busy moving from a rental farm to the 120 acre place he purchased in Grove Township. Over the years William and Mary acquired eight children and an additional 600 acres. An 1875 sketch of his farmstead shows a spacious two-story house amidst mature shade trees, an orchard, both beef and dairy cattle, draft animals, light-harness horses for the family carriage. His well-kept outbuildings included a large, three story barn. Built European-style into a sloping hillside, the stone foundation comprised a partly below-grade space for winter protection. Above the main level was a cavernous hayloft.

William started farming several years before Peter. He had the advantage of farming during the war years, when prices for grain and pork and beef were high. While Peter's estate would soon exceed that of his older brother, William nevertheless did quite well. When he died local newspapers wrote that he was *"signally successful," "one of the best-known men in the county," "ranked as one of the wealthiest men in the area."*

In his lifetime, though, news articles about him were generally less laudatory and more humorous than those written about Peter. The one that appears below makes light of what was a bad situation.

Under the headline "A Narrow Escape," the Telegraph carried this article on March 3, 1880:

*Wm. Hopley took a lot of cattle to Omaha recently, and on Saturday night went into a car with a lantern where a bull was tied. As he went to pass the bull made a lunge for him and caught his body between the horns and pressed him against the side of the car. The room between the bull's head and the side of the car was uncomfortably scant, and to make Mr. Hopley realize his position more fully, the bull commenced to churning him up and down, his head striking on the roof of the car. Presently a man came along, peeped into the car, and, supposing no earthly power could save the situation, shouted good-bye and left.*

*When the bull stepped back and blowed his nose preparatory to another plunge, Mr. Hopley dropped to the floor. As the bull was tied he managed to crawl away from him. He is badly bruised but is able to attend to business.*

William had dairy cows, and also Herford cattle. His bulls were purebred stock. Regardless of the breed, there was a reason this animal was being sent to slaughter with a sturdy rope attached to a ring in his nose. A horned bull turned vicious is a deadly beast. William Hopley was fortunate not to have met with serious injury, or even death.

The editor who wrote the story knew William. To cover it in the offhand manner he did indicates good humor on the part of both men.

During early December of 1895, Cass County was visited by a number of Indians who were supposed to be living in the Omaha area. They were probably of the Ioway tribe (use whichever spelling you prefer), or Pottawattamie, although news articles do not so state. The group camped out near Atlantic and was, for a few days, an object of much curiosity. Political correctness not being an issue, people came from miles to gawk. One young man was so forward as to try to touch a "squaw" on the arm. The reaction was not good, it was written, as offense was taken by a defender of the woman. The Indian, the article continued, was able to kick and was *"handy with a hatchet."* No harm was done, and Indians proceeded to call on local residents, *"relieving them of anything they had to give away."*

One of those who received a visit was William Hopley. Hopley was in a benevolent mood, having just finished picking corn. The Indian, apparently strolling about by himself, was interested in a meal. Hopley invited him inside for dinner. What Mary thought of the guest was not recorded. The Indian ate heartily. While preparing to leave he asked William for fifty cents.

Hopley found this richly amusing, and thought the Telegraph should know. He'd not only given an Indian his dinner, he'd paid half a dollar for the privilege.

William Hopley's humor was further illustrated in a news report that appeared only months before his death. In November of 1907 he went to Rochester, Minnesota, for surgery on the leg tumor that had plagued him painfully for years. Before departing he was interviewed. The article said he had twice previously undergone surgery but had experienced "*only temporary relief. Of late the tumor has been growing like a mushroom.*" The front page feature in the Atlantic Democrat continued:

*Talking to a Democrat reporter, Mr. Hopley said the operation, which will be performed at the Catholic hospital in Rochester is suggested to be a part of his desire to treat several religions fairly and equitably. The first operation on the leg was at a Methodist hospital in Chicago. The second was in a Presbyterian hospital and this, as stated previously, will be at a Catholic hospital. Mr. Hopley insinuated that if his leg and money held out he would go down the balance of the line and give all denominations of hospitals a chance at him.*

Hopley also related an experience he had during one of his earlier hospital stays. He shared a room with another patient. He arose early one morning and started to dress. He found the pants leg much too tight and feared the tumor had ballooned overnight. He was about to "*sound the fire alarm*" when he realized he was trying to squeeze into someone else's trousers.

His wife, Mary Okell Hopley, had died young in 1884. She left seven children ranging in age from Jennie, 19, to Frank, who was 9. Jennie was followed by two other daughters. Then, in 1869, a son, Thomas, after which came two more girls. Frank was born in 1875. English custom held the first son as heir, at least in terms of carrying on. There are indications William was closer to his oldest son than he was to Frank, who was out of the Hopley family arrangement for decades.

When Mary died Jennie took over household duties. She would continue for a few years, departing to be replaced by younger sister Mabel. Jennie never married and her social life was limited. She did, however, have an occasional party, one of which is described in the following article taken from the Telegraph of August 29, 1891:

*A large party was given Friday evening by the Misses and Thomas Hopley at the residence of their father, Mr. Wm. Hopley, of about three miles south of the city. The larger number of guests was from this city and Lewis and the surrounding country was excellently represented. Although several carriage loads of guests succeeded in getting lost along the way, all arrived by 9 o'clock. Games of cards, table croquet, and other amusements were indulged in until 10 o'clock, when refreshments of high order were served, after which several couples enjoyed several round dances. Everyone present was highly entertained by the hosts and report one of the best times of the season.*

When her younger sister, Blanch, took a husband in 1893, Jennie and other sisters saw to it that the house was looking grand. The Lewis paper published a lengthy article lauding the event, *"which was held in the Hopley mansion in Grove Township."* The wedding party included sister Mattie (Martha), who was then twenty-six and single.

Mattie was not well, suffering from consumption. She sought relief in New Mexico and Arizona (we don't know, but one or more of Peter's frequent trips to Arizona might have included his niece, or a visit to her). Mattie gave up on Arizona and returned to what newspapers referred to as *"the Hopley mansion in Grove Township."* In doing so she turned for treatment to Dr. Cassius Lightner Campbell.

Dr. Campbell could do her no more good than her stay in Arizona, and Mattie expired as did the year 1896. Her funeral, held in the home, was on New Year's Day of 1897. Two years later Dr. Campbell married William's third daughter, Sophia. Another fine wedding might have been celebrated in a fine Hopley home, but was not. Sophia and the doctor eloped. In late December the following appeared in the Telegraph:

*Dr. C.L. Campbell and Miss Sophia Hopley were married Wednesday, Dec. 21, at the home of Miss Hopley's sister, Mrs. Roberts, in Rippey. The doctor was very quiet about the affair and facts of the case hard to obtain. Miss Hopley has been teaching school in Des Moines and returned there after a short visit home. The doctor quietly took a train to Audubon Tuesday morning and from there went to Rippey, in Greene County. After the ceremony they left for Chicago and other points for three weeks, after which time they will return to Atlantic and make their home at the John Scott property at 403 West 6th Street. Mr. and Mrs. Campbell are well known to our readers. The bride is the well-known and accomplished daughter of William Hopley and the groom is a partner in the firm of Campbell and Porterfield, physicians and surgeons.*

Marriage represented an abrupt change in lifestyle for Dr. Campbell. He was born in Pennsylvania in 1856, attended several medical schools, graduating from Miami Medical College in Cincinnati in 1881. He returned to his home state and practiced for a couple of years, then decided to go west. Doctor Campbell settled in Lewis in 1883, remaining there until moving his practice to Atlantic in 1897.

He was, at the time of his marriage, 43 years old. He and Sophia rented a home for a short time, then lived for a few years in a relatively modest house on Locust Street. Sophia had grown up in the splendid farm home of her parents, and Dr. Campbell was a man of financial substance. He had an office in various Atlantic locations, partnered at times with another doctor. He and Sophia eventually moved to a much larger residence at 611 Poplar. The place was roomy enough for their residence, to accommodate his office, and have a room or two in which patients could receive short or, at least in the case of relatives, long-term care. Dr. Campbell and his wife were much relied on by ailing members of the family.

William's estate peaked at about 1,000 acres. Of the Hopley brothers, only Peter had more land. There should have been room on William's farm for both sons. Apparently there was not, and there are few clues as to why.

We find frequent items in both Lewis and Atlantic papers associating William and Thomas. *William and his oldest son bought a load cattle. William and Thomas Hopley have now finished picking corn. William and Thomas Hopley accompanied a railroad car full of hogs to the market in Chicago.* If Frank, who was only six years younger than Thomas, was a part of these trips or deals, the papers neglected to so mention.

Frank left the farm early, probably right after high school. He worked a series of odd jobs, found permanent employment at the Iowa

School for the Deaf in Council Bluffs. Shortly after he was married in 1902 he rented a farm in Audubon County. Later, in 1908 (the year William died), he and his young family moved to South Dakota.

William, fighting a losing battle with the leg tumor, wrote a will naming Thomas and Jennie as executors. Thomas was given complete rights of farm management. Whether this strained his relationship with his younger brother we don't know. We do know that Thomas, who was socially active, visited friends and relatives in various locations. These visits were duly noted by one or more local newspapers. He and Jennie bought land in South Dakota, but we find no mention that he ever went to that state to see his brother, and neither were Frank and family in the custom of returning to the home place.

Jennie, a few years after her father passed, moved to Atlantic. Thomas remained on the farm, with Mabel taking over household responsibilities. Jennie boarded with Dr. and Mrs. Campbell. Census records of 1900 and 1910 show her as employed by the doctor as an accountant. In addition to sending bills and collecting payments, she probably served as receptionist and helped with patients and housework. Although she went to school only through 8$^{th}$ grade, in 1915 she attended a business college. Jennie was also involved in several real estate transactions not long after her father died (in 1908). Newspaper accounts say she bought a lot next to Sophia and Dr. Campbell, hired an architect from Omaha, then apparently either built or remodeled a house. At about this time brother Thomas was wheeling and dealing with William's estate. He may have been trying to emulate Uncle Peter, who was repeatedly making the news for one deal or another. Thomas bought, sold, traded. He was also the object of a few lawsuits. For this reason some of the property transfers involving Jennie may have been an ownership change in name only, performed to protect Thomas.

Jennie's house at 621 Poplar must not have worked out for her. By 1920 she was listed as a nurse, living as a boarder at "the Cavanaugh's." By 1925 she was back on the farm, again doing household duties for her brother, Thomas.

# Chapter Ten

A notable aspect of news articles about Hopley is that Atlantic papers, for decades, referred to Hopley farms "of Atlantic," or as being "south of Atlantic." The Lewis paper was more accurate—Peter and Harry's mailing address was Lewis and their land was closer to the smaller town. When Peter and Edna built the mansion in Lewis, Atlantic editors so acknowledged. His farm, however, remained "south of Atlantic." Pretty much every paper in the county covered the building of the house, the water supply, installation of gas lighting. When the furnace was installed shortly after the turn of the century the news made page one in Lewis and was reprinted elsewhere. Even the barn was newsworthy. When Peter gave his children a Shetland pony the papers so announced, and the Lewis paper took note a few months later when he acquired a dog, apparently a big one, as it was trained to pull a cart.

Richard Muffley, of Arlington, Virginia, remembers his grandmother Minnie talking about the ponies (hers was named Barney). Each of Peter and Edna's children had their own. Some parents might have expected their youngsters to share, but not the Hopleys. Even taking into consideration the age difference, that one daughter died too young to have a pony, there still must have been seven or eight at any one time. The horse barn in the country was enormous—the one in town had to be spacious as well.

In Peter Hopley local news reporters found a man whose tales of the old and wild west were entertaining, as were his European horse-buying ventures. He was a self-made man, a Capitalist in a country that, for the most part, celebrated Capitalism. When Peter maintained that he'd inherited nothing of monetary value, there is no reason to question him. While his parents had money when they left England, made more of it here, the family was large. His mother, known by friends as "grandma Hopley," lived thirty years longer than his father. There was probably little left in her estate when she passed on in 1902, and her sons—at least in the case of William and Peter—didn't need it anyway. They may, in fact, have contributed to her support during her final years.

Peter Hopley, in a span of a decade, made a great deal of money. He built on this to make even more. By the turn of the century there were wealthier men in Cass County, but not many. Of them, few were as colorful. They didn't run around with Buffalo Bill, show Suffolk Punch stallions, have friends in England and Scotland, drop into consulates in Germany, win Arizona land in a card game, and would never own a vineyard in California.

By 1903 Hopley, at the age of fifty-six, was arguably Cass County's most widely-known resident. That local papers covered him so closely is not surprising, but their stories were often reprinted in Council Bluffs, Omaha and Des Moines. Reporters from those cities made trips to Lewis, or at least phone calls. When Hopley offered advice on farming or investment or saving his words (often attributed to a "successful southwest Iowa farmer" who was not named) could be found in papers published in Wisconsin, Minnesota, Missouri, Illinois and elsewhere. In January he made a hog-buying trip to North Dakota. Atlantic and Lewis newspapers felt the public wanted to know. While there he sent home word of a mishap. He and several others were traveling from one town to another in a horse-drawn coach. The weather was bitterly cold and a strong north wind was howling. On a particularly exposed stretch of road a particularly strong gust of wind blew the coach off the traveled portion, where it was temporarily out of service. The experience must have reminded Hopley of Colorado in the 1860s. Someone thought the newspapers would be interested, and they printed the story. Editors printed another for no other reason than to announce he'd arrived home.

While Hopley was buying hogs in North Dakota, the Atlantic Telegraph and Atlantic Democrat were having one of their periodic spats. Newly elected state and federal politicians were taking office. Some were in favor of protective measures that would lessen the financial peaks and valleys of farming and livestock production. The Republican paper, the News Telegraph, had one view, the Democrat newspaper another. Both sought to use Peter Hopley as an example to support their position. The Telegraph, knowing Hopley's politics and anticipating his objection to government control, interviewed him first.

Hopley had just lost a bundle on cattle (he uses the figure $10,000, something akin to dropping close to half a million today). He didn't boast about it, but came close, saying he expected to break even. He was covered, he said, as when he sensed the cattle market going sour he invested in hogs. Each newspaper applied their own spin   While Hopley seems not to have been in favor of price supports, the Democrat cited his experience to illustrate that a lot of money could be lost. Not everyone had the flexibility, and foresight, of Peter Hopley. A safety net should, in the view of The Democrat, be put in place.

A few weeks later an article appeared informing readers that the "Hopley School," four miles south of Atlantic, was now open. None of Peter and Edna's nor William and Mary's children attended—only a couple were still in school and they went elsewhere—but there were enough Hopley hired men with families to merit the name.

Later the same year a peculiar and unexplained article informed readers that *"Peter Hopley is not a pro sprinter, but says he can get lost easier, walk faster, make better time at night than any other Englishman of his height. His midnight jaunt to Walnut leads us to believe this to be true."* The story was one of those the paper felt needed no explain.

An accident covered in much more detail made the front page of the Telegraph in July of 1913 while his wife, Edna, was visiting their married daughter living in Idaho. The victim was Peter Hopley, nationally known horseman. He would have preferred to have kept this account out of the papers. Below the headline *"HORSE BACKS BUGGY INTO RIVER"* we read this:

*Peter Hopley left a week ago today for Europe, where he will buy horses, which will be shipped here to restock his farm. The day before he left he was the main figure in an accident which occurred on his farm. He had driven down to the river on his farm to oversee some hired men, while they were catching up some hogs to be shipped. While he was sitting in the buggy which was in the driveway near the river bank, he decided to turn the horse and buggy around. During this process the horse was compelled to back up a short distance, and when Hopley got ready for the horse to go ahead it kept right on backing. Peter exercised his lung capacity to the utmost, using the whip with his sturdy right arm, but failed to stop the horse in his backward trip. Finally the river back was reached and into the water went buggy, man, and horse. The buggy was under the horse and Mr. Hopley was under both. His son, Harry Hopley, and two hired men were compelled to hitch a team onto a rope which they tied around the neck of the struggling horse and pulled the horse and buggy out, after which Peter was helped to shore in a very wet and bedraggled condition. He had no need of medical aid, however, in order to free his lungs of the water which he had imbibed, as he was equal to the occasion. The ducking did him no harm, nor did it prevent him from leaving for Europe on the next day. It is said, however, that Peter will probably not attempt to turn that horse around in a smaller area than a forty acre field. Peter was not what you might call proud of that particular escapade and told no one about it, hence the reason for this story not appearing sooner.*

In 1913, before the river was straightened, the distance from the top of the bank to water was generally less than it is today. Hopley's plunge was probably only a few feet, a factor in the absence of injury. Regardless, the fact that a man who had built a reputation, and a fortune, on horses was treated in such a manner by one he had chosen for his personal use was too much for the paper to pass up, even though the editor didn't learn of the incident until two weeks later.

Peter Hopley played a role in the routing of what would be, from 1910 until the coming of the Interstate system fifty years later, a much-used state highway across Iowa. The State Highway Commission, formed just six years earlier, was working on designating a route from river to river. With a hodge-podge of trails and dirt roads to choose from, they debated the best between Des Moines and Council Bluffs. Charles Willey, editor and owner of the Lewis Standard and a man with a keen interest in seeing the road pass through his town, attended a meeting held by the "State Good Roads Committee" in Council Bluffs in April of 1910. Among those representing Cass County and Lewis interests was Peter Hopley. Their concern was the route from Atlantic to Oakland, which could have gone more or less straight west from Atlantic to Hancock, then south to Oakland. Hopley argued that a better choice would be from Atlantic to Lewis, then west past what is now known as the Hitchcock House, then on to Oakland (essentially the White Pole Road, but not the course of Highway 6, which came later). Atlantic representatives supported this route out of good will—the road would go through their town regardless. Lewis was the big stakeholder, and Peter Hopley stood to benefit from a better road by his place as well. He offered to maintain the portion that passed through his land (which he probably did anyway) until such time as the state had the funding to do so. The committee thought this sounded good, voted accordingly, and adjourned. Willey, who didn't particularly care what route was taken from Oakland to Council Bluffs, said that matter would be taken up another day.

Remarks attributed to Peter indicate he himself could be content with modest surroundings. He had, however, no reluctance to spend lavishly—particularly on the women in his life. The home he built in Lewis, the Hopley mansion, was statelier than William's. It would eventually go to ruin, in part, because of what it was. The house was what Edna wanted. It was consistent with the opulent life style of the rich during what Mark Twain called "the gilded age." The house served the family well. For those who followed, though, it was too big, too elaborate, too expensive to maintain.

During the Edna Hopley years the house was more than a home—it was the hub of social events held on a scale difficult to imagine in Lewis today. And even the most routine coming and going rated mention in the papers.

Peter's sister, Hannah, along with her husband, Henry, came to visit in 1883, the year before the Hopley home in Lewis was built. Henry and

Hannah Wormsley had, by that time, accumulated a fortune, built one of the most elegant homes in Denver and would outdo it when they moved to California. Newspapers made mention of the fact that Henry, one of the richest men in Denver, had gotten his start in the wholesale meat business as a butcher in Lewis. (The Wormsely's would visit numerous times during the late 1800s and early 1900s. Not many people who called on Peter and Edna Hopley had a greater net worth, but Henry and Hannah did.)

In mid-September, 1887, two family members made the front page on the same day.

*Peter Hopley returned last evening from a trip through Wyoming and Montana. He said the corn through Nebraska is unusually promising.*

Below the fold we find this:

*Misses Allie Childs and Nelle Walker and Miss Edith Hopley of Lewis left last evening for Mt. Vernon to attend college. Miss Hopley will take a special course in music.*

What must have been a pleasant assignment for newspaper reporters, an event that offers a view of the Hopley family, the house, and their lifestyle, took place when Margaret was married in the fall of 1900.

She was then twenty-three years of age, college educated; a popular and a most attractive young lady. Her older sister, Beulah, had died five years earlier at the age of twenty. This left Margaret the oldest living child and, it would seem, a favorite of her father (she was named for Peter's older sister). The announcement of her wedding was an important social news item. It seems likely that most of those who knew the Hopley family coveted an invitation. A late-summer item in the *Lewis Standard* relayed word that, as Margaret wished to have the wedding take place in the home of her parents, the guest list would necessarily be limited. Apparently the mansion could only comfortably accommodate about 250 people.

Charles Willey was just beginning with the *Lewis Standard* and the wedding was an opportunity for him to meet potential subscribers. The paper's owner, G.W.B. Fletcher, probably went as well. The event had been planned for months; preparation was extensive and detailed.

The evening of September 11 was pleasant. Reporters from several newspapers joined the throng of invited guests. Oregon Street was lined with parked carriages. Attendees arriving in the early-evening darkness were greeted by an outdoor array of gas lighting. The Hopleys, it seemed to those who entered the mansion, had everything.

When reporters boasted that Lewis had rarely been the site of such a grand affair, they were not overstating the case.

*One of the happiest events of the season occurred at the spacious home of Mr. and Mrs. Peter Hopley of Lewis on Tuesday evening, September 11. It was the marriage of their oldest daughter, Margaret Imogene, to Frank Whitman Lumsden of Valley Junction.*

*The bay window was festooned with pink and white ribbons intermingled with beautiful flowers while the back ground was banked with potted plants and ferns. The lamps on either side cast a rose hue over the whole, presenting a veritable fairy land. The entire house was prettily decorated with American beauties, carnations, and ferns, while the veranda and lawn were illuminated with beautifully colored lights.*

*Promptly at eight o'clock Miss Edith Martin took her place at the piano where her beautiful and light fantastic touch brought forth the strains of Mendelssohn's wedding march, while at a signal from Miss Jennie Roush, the bridal party appeared at the top of the stairway. First came the ribbon girls, the Misses Margaret Kemp and Mabel Hopley, each daintily robed in blue gowns carrying white and pink carnations. An aisle was formed from the foot of the stairs to the altar. Following them came the groom and best man, Mr. Chas. Waldon of Valley Junction, both dressed in conventional black. Then came the bridesmaids, Miss Alberta Vance of Kellogg, Helen True of Eddyville, Birdie Downs of Atlantic, and Rose Rickey of Griswold, clad in pink and blue gowns and carrying pink and red roses, then came the Maid of Honor, Miss Eda Hopley, sister of the bride, dressed in green and carrying white roses. Leaning on her father's arm came the bride, dressed in a beautiful gown of white satin, trimmed with real lace, carrying a large bouquet of bride's roses and wearing a tuelia veil adorned with diamonds and agates.*

*During the marriage ceremony the couple stood under a lover's knot of pink and white roses. After congratulations, the party was summoned to the bridal table in an adjoining room which was connected to the main dining room by large double doors where fifty plates were laid at one time. Each guest was presented with favors of goldenrod. The supper was an elaborate affair, the tables nearly groaning under the weight of rare delicacies. The bridal table was beautifully decorated with smilax, ferns and tule roses, the center piece being a massive decoration of pink and white roses arranged diagonally across the table terminating in large bows, while on either side of the table were arranged silver candelabras holding pink candles, with silken shades to match. The event was among the most elegant ever held in Lewis.*
*(Atlantic News-Telegraph, September 13, 1900.)*

The article concludes with a brief depiction of various—and quite exquisite—wedding gifts. The cost of the wedding, excluding gifts, would have fed the town of Lewis for months.

Other Hopley girls were married in the house. Edna married Edward Askew in November of 1908, less than two months after her uncle William had died. The couple spoke their vows in *"the bay window of the drawing room of the Hopley home, which was banked with palms and a beautiful wedding bell."* Edna was wearing her mother's silk wedding gown and was attended by her twin sisters, Mary and Minnie.

A bit more than a year later, in June of 1910, the Hopley mansion was the site of another family occasion. Edward and Edna's first child, Peter Hopley Askew, was christened in front of the same bay window. He was, The Standard revealed, *"Christened with water from the River Jordan, which had been sent by friends from Europe for the occasion."*

In between those events—Edna's marriage in 1908 and the christening her son in 1910--certain ladies of Lewis formed what was called the Crescent Club. Their purpose, as stated in by-laws, included the enjoyment of social activities. They became an influential group and would do much good. With their dues they rented space for a Lewis Public library, bought books, served as the first librarians, pursued other literary endeavors. They were also quite social and engaged in activities they found pleasurable. Membership was limited to twenty-five women. When a vacancy occurred the potential replacement was voted upon in an "informal" (unrecorded) manner. This assured that if an applicant was denied, she could not check the minutes and see who voted against her.

Mrs. Peter Hopley, during the 1890s and early 1900s, was perhaps the most socially active woman in Lewis. We find her hosting card parties for dozens of guests, of either beginning or concluding these afternoons with two and three course luncheons. She entertained often and lavishly. She had a servant, a part-time cook, a gardener and, with the coming of the automobile, a Studebaker and a hired chauffeur. She could speak with experience about travel in Europe, throughout the United States, of theater and style and culture.

A typical month in her social life took place in June of 1908. She and two married daughters, Edna and Edith, were guests at an "eight-course breakfast" held for about thirty ladies and hosted by a Mrs. Burk and Mrs. Spangler in Atlantic (this raises an obvious question: what would the courses be in an eight-course breakfast? We wish the reporter would have been more complete). The following week, Edna Hopley entertained several ladies from Marne. The gala event of the month took place on June 23rd. Mrs. Peter Hopley, along with Mrs. Lucy Harris, Mrs. Edna Hopley Askew and Mrs. Edith Hopley Hedges hosted, in the Hopley mansion, a reception to which 175 socially prominent women of Cass County were invited. The house was ornately decorated with fresh roses and ferns, Lewis ladies named Misses Zeta Ally (the last name "Ally" appeared in the papers, but it probably should have been Allyn) and Minnie Albright attended the "frappe bowl," a delicate and delicious lunch was served to all in attendance, and a most enjoyable time was had. While a few table games were played, most of the afternoon was spent in cordial conversation and strolls through the extensive Hopley garden. The cereus was not in bloom, but the roses and iris were.

Most of the Atlantic ladies came by rail. The conductor, according to the Telegraph, was considerate enough to hold the northbound train. Scheduled to depart Lewis at 4:30, the train delayed until 5:30 that afternoon in order to take ladies who had attended the party home. Other passengers, we assume, were not amused.

It was in this environment the Lewis Crescent Club was formed. Edna Hopley, at the center of Lewis society, was not, and never became, a member. We can only speculate. She may have considered Crescent beneath her, may not have felt she had time, may have had some personal animosity toward club organizers. On the other hand, it is possible that Crescent Club was created by women who were not part of Edna's inner circle, and chose to create one of their own.

Mary Hopley was the club's first secretary. Della Forsythe Hopley, Edna's daughter-in-law, was an early member who would hold several offices, including president, and would become an honorary member. Edna, though, until the day she died, either shunned, or was shunned by, Crescent Club.

In 1911, a year after the Christening of Edna's son, yet another memorable event took place in the Hopley mansion. The twins, Mary and Minnie, were brides in a double wedding.

*"At high noon today at the Congregational Church occurred the marriage of the misses Mary and Minnie Hopley, twin sisters, the youngest children of Peter and Edna Hopley, to James Patton Harris, son of Mr. and Mrs. W.J. Harris of Lewis, and Fred C. Muffley, of Soldier, Idaho, respectively."* (Atlantic Daily Telegraph, June 17, 1911.)

(Newspapers do make mistakes. Minnie and Mary were not the youngest children. Gertrude was born after them, as was Wayland.)

Following the wedding more than two hundred guests attended the reception in the mansion. Once again the first story was decorated with dozens upon dozens of roses and carnations, ferns and ribbons, and long tables were set with fine silver and china. In the kitchen hired help prepared the meal—a three-course luncheon—and more hired help did the serving. One news article informed readers that *"due to the prominence of Mr. Hopley, who established the Riverside Farm, the wedding attracted attention from all parts of the state. . . "*

Both couples left that night for Chicago, then went by boat to Duluth, where they spent two weeks. James Harris, who was cashier in his father's bank, then returned with his wife to Lewis. Minnie and Fred Muffley went on to his home in Idaho.

Edna went with them, "planning to stay indefinitely." Having one's mother move in just days after the wedding may have been a bit awkward. The Muffleys however, apparently didn't mind. Their first child was born the following March. (Mary was not in the best of health at the time of her marriage. She had, for some time, experienced heart trouble. She died in 1915.)

The parties at the Hopley mansion went on and on. Edna entertained, entertained and entertained some more. When a daughter visited receptions were certain to follow. As her youngest son, Wayland, progressed through high school the passage from one grade to another was cause for an event in the Hopley mansion. Della entertained, and when Edna wasn't co-hosting an event with Lucy Harris she teamed with her daughter-in-law. The Titanic went down in April of 1912. This was no doubt a subject of conversation as Edna attended and hosted several receptions that month, usually for groups of 30 or more. In late May she and Della teamed up, on Memorial Day weekend, to hold a dinner party at which 80 ladies were in attendance. Only illness slowed Edna down, and only when she was gone did gala parties in the mansion cease.

Four years after his wife's death, Peter gave the house to Margaret. She and her husband were by then established in Storm Lake, had no intention of returning to Lewis. The house, though, had been her childhood home, the site of her wedding. Peter wanted her to have it. The document transferring ownership was signed in 1923. If was not, however, filed until after Peter's death three years later. The senior Hopley would continue to live there, retaining a housekeeper and a gardener to keep the place in order, for the remainder of his days.

Margaret kept the house just a year, then sold it. Timing and location were not in the house's favor. A home of that size and style was of less interest to a buyer in Lewis that it would have been in a larger town. Two years after the sale the Depression set in, and a good share of the Lewis business district died. Twenty years after Peter Hopley's death the house was showing signs of disrepair. Into the 1950s the slippage continued; the place needed paint, roof and window repair. The house would eventually set vacant, targeted by vandals. Walnut woodwork, portions of the banister from the grand staircase, fireplace mantles, were stolen. Stained glass was broken, pigeons and bats littered the upstairs bedrooms. The once plush carpet was tattered, the massive front door, through which many of the most highly-regarded area citizens of the time had passed, was nailed shut. Those seeking entry were able, however, to do so through a back door or broken window.

Margaret passed away in California in 1957. If she ever returned to Lewis, saw her childhood home, the sight must have been heartbreaking. What may have once been the grandest house in Lewis was torn down by Miller Cavin, a Lewis carpenter. His son, Steve, then a teen-ager, helped dismantle the building. He remembers spacious rooms, high ceilings, three bathrooms, marble sinks, intricate hard-wood floors of slender oak slats trimmed with walnut in a parquet pattern. (The carpet was added after Margaret sold the house. Edna would never have allowed her gorgeous, carefully selected hardwood to be slandered by garish red carpet.) The kitchen, although connected to the rear of the two-story house, was essentially a separate one-story structure. This was the preference in houses of this type, keeping kitchen heat, and the servants, at a distance.

Miller Cavin re-used the lumber in other building projects, including a home built for one of his sons.

# Chapter Eleven

The two boys, Harry and Wayland, had a much different youth than did their father.

*"Mrs. Hopley and I have reared a family of nine children and given them all a good education. For several years we have given them most of the money we have made, as well as part of our fortune. A man my age doesn't need much, neither does my wife. We believe it is better to give the children money from time to time instead of waiting until we are gone."*

The same Peter Hopley who professed that hard work, long hours, frugality and a willingness to take risks was the key to success gave liberally of his earnings and "part of our fortune" to his offspring. A man who attended school only briefly, had instead learned his lessons at home, with his mother's tutelage, through experience and a self-imposed discipline of study, did not expect anything approaching the same commitment from his children. Harry went to Knox College in Illinois. He excelled in football. After graduation he joined the Maroons, Atlantic's semi-pro football team.

It was written of Harry that he and his father were extremely close. He was the oldest son and, to Peter, represented the future of Hopley farms.

With his first three children being daughters, Peter may have had some anxiety regarding who would farm Hopley land when he was gone. With the birth of Harry, that question was answered. Newspaper articles tell us young Harry accompanied his father everywhere. Like his older sisters he attended school in Lewis. During the summer and on weekends he went with Peter to the farm, to stock shows, accompanied him when he called on the bank. Peter called on the banks often and would, in fact, become part owner and vice president in one. Cash flow issues in an operation as big as Hopley's mandated borrowing. He was, even before Harry was born, raising hundreds of his own calves to fatten. When, however, he saw feeders going at a price he felt was favorable, he did not hesitate to buy a carload or more. Relying heavily on borrowed money was a system that worked well for Peter and Harry.

Harry, the darling of his older sisters, was fourteen when his only brother, Wayland, was born. The age difference was such that by the time Wayland was old enough to become active on the farm Harry was in college. The two would later farm adjoining land, work together and get along, but did not exactly grow up together.

Harry Hopley graduated from college in 1903. He played football, farmed with his father, owned fine horses, and drove a stylish carriage. While Harry had much given to him, he was close to Peter, saw his father work, and learned. Peter had high expectations for Harry, the oldest son, and seems to have conveyed them well. Harry responded with a work ethic and initiative. He joined his father as a manager and overseer. He could have coasted, left most of the heavy decision-making to Peter. Instead he set about buying a farm of his own.

Harry was a fine horseman, knew cattle, worked hard but not so hard it stood in the way of a good time. The years following college must have been enjoyable ones. He had money and status, good looks that included an athlete's physique and a swath of thick, dark Hopley hair. He was an eligible and prized catch, and he was in no hurry. He dated a number of local ladies, not deciding on one until he was twenty-eight years old.

Before taking a bride he acquired land that adjoined his father's on the west, and called it "West Side Farm."

In the fall of 1908, below an article stating that the Atlantic Canning Company was running full time, but would not put up as much sweet corn as usual because acreage was down, we find a hint that Harry's status as a man about-the-county was about to change. The following appeared in the Telegraph on September 11, 1908:

*The Lewis Standard says there is something suspicious about Harry Hopley making a lot of improvements in his residence on the West Side Farm located north of Lewis. The dining room has been enlarged and remodeled: a new furnace is being installed: and lights will be furnished from a complete gas plant. The remodeled residence will be equipped with an up to date water system. New floors will be put down. The flooring is only 7/8 of an inch wide, slivers almost. All of which makes it look as if Ethan Allen and Jack Colwell will soon have an opportunity to toot their whistles in earnest.*

The Telegraph waited a few weeks, then in late December followed up by sending a reporter of their own to West Side Farm. The house was said to be a brick building, older but substantial. A striking open stairway was nearing completion, as was a roomy front porch and an "ornate balustrade." (The house on Harry's "West Side Farm" was ¼ mile or so west of the East Nishnabotna. The home Wayland later built for Helen was on the east side of the river and a mile north, near where Peter and Edna had originally lived. After Harry died in 1945, Wayland and Helen moved into the house, Wayland Jr., who was then 21 years old, moved into what had been his parent's home.)

The article concluded by saying the extensive renovation was to prepare for the soon-to-be mistress, who was *"the most bewitching of Cass County's fair daughters."*

Four months later Harry and Della Forsythe were married.

*At the home of H.K. Forsythe of Griswold at noon today Miss Della Forsythe and Harry Hopley were married.*

Following a description of the ceremony, the article continued:

*The groom is the junior partner in the firm of Peter Hopley & Son, and is one of the hustling young business men of the area. He is a splendid young man and everyone who knows him likes him. He is, in every way, worthy of the young woman who has taken him in marriage. The couple will leave Griswold this evening on the Burlington for an extended trip through the southwest. Upon return they will take up residence in the beautiful new abode the groom has built on the Hopley farms north of Lewis.*

The article concluded on a wistful note: *The News joins the hosts of friends of the contracting party in wishing them the best this old world affords and to hope that their pathway in life might be strewn with flowers. (Atlantic Telegraph February 28, 1909)*

Old Peter had concise words of advice for young people: *"Cut out the extravagances, work for yourself, put enthusiasm and energy into your work, study all you can, save the big portion of what you earn, then you will not have to envy the man who started as you did and passed you early in the race."*

Harry, even as he gave his bride a home that rivaled the one his parents had worked and saved for years to build, seemed to understand. He knew his parents at an age when they were living what they preached. The boys who followed did not.

# Chapter Twelve

William Hopley's son-in-law was a man he may have seen more often professionally than socially. William, in his later years, suffered increasingly from what was probably a malignant tumor. Over a period of ten years Dr. Campbell tried various treatments. All failed to give permanent relief. Specialists were consulted. As has previously been noted, several surgeries were performed, incapacitating him for extended periods. Thomas, nearing thirty years of age, took over farm management in the mid-1890s. Based on what we know of his business transactions, the productivity of the farm deteriorated after Thomas acquired it.

In the late summer of 1908, with the corn too tall to cultivate, with hay in the barn, Peter gave responsibility for his place to his 25-year-old son, Harry, and made his annual horse-buying expedition to Europe. Either shortly before or after his departure, William was hospitalized in Omaha. On about the first of September he was released and taken by his daughter, Sophia, into the home she shared with Dr. Campbell. William, who had promised that if "his leg and his money held out" he'd have an operation in a hospital carrying the name of every religious denomination, didn't achieve that goal. He died in his daughter's home on September 12.

William's will, prepared just days before his death, was plain: Thomas and Jennie were to be administrators of his will and the farm.

Things would continue, the will directed, *"under the management of Thomas Hopley, a son and one of the administrators."* An annual distribution was to be made of profits derived, *"but no final distribution has been made and none desired at this time, each of said heirs retaining a common and equal and undivided interest in the entire estate."*

The will listed William's assets; about 800 acres of farm land, 165 head of cattle, 1 bull, 38 horses, 1 stallion, 1 mule, 150 hogs, 500 bushel of oats, 400 bushel of timothy seed and 125 tons of hay—some stacked, some in the barn. He also owned several lots in Atlantic, including 5 rental houses. There was a certificate of deposit in the Atlantic National bank in the amount of $1000, 4 shares of stock in the Shrine Temple in Des Moines, 1 share of Atlantic Northern and Southern Railroad, and 45 shares of American Pneumatic Services.

The next generation, although with what may have been less than complete harmony, had taken over the William Hopley operation.

Peter, in Europe, could not be contacted. He did not learn of his brother's death until he returned several weeks later. While the news could not have been a shock, it was an occasion for thoughts and memories, to mourn the mortality of himself and those with whom his life mingled. The older brother who had worked to secure passage for Peter and Ann, who took them to Iowa, had a successful and growing farm operation when Peter returned from the west; an example, a man who set the bar Peter would vault, was no longer.

William died owning close to a thousand acres and considerable other property. Peter had twice that and was still expanding. William built the mansion in Grove Township. Peter outdid it with an even grander mansion in Lewis. William's children, some of them, did not continue schooling after eighth grade. Peter's all attended college. William's daughters, those that married, had fine weddings. Peter and Edna's were feted at gala events local papers rated as the "most impressive ever held in Lewis." Mary Okell Hopley did not even attempt to compete with her sister-in-law on a social basis.

Peter vowed he would outdo the nameless boys who taunted him in school. If William, in Peter's mind, represented them, he made good on his promise.

It was at about the time of William's death that Peter, on a horse-buying journeys to Europe, purchased a few cattle of the "Scottish Shorthorn" breed. Harry, then in his mid-twenties and farming partly with his father, partly on his own, liked the cattle. He and Peter began having annual sales of purebred breeding stock. These events were said to be strictly business while old Peter was in charge. We might suspect otherwise, but have no first-hand accounts. Changes would come later—from horses and Shorthorns to Herefords to Angus and hogs, and from presumably staid affairs to multi-day parties hosted by Wayland and Helen at which potential buyers were put in the proper frame of mind by abundant amounts barbeque. The liquor was free, and there was plenty of it.

Peter Hopley, at the age of 67, made his last horse-buying trip to Europe. Turmoil was building, World War 1 in the offing, and good draft horses—if they could be found—were at a premium. Hopley went anyway. He was accompanied by "Doc" Forsythe of Griswold.

Henry K. Forsythe was then a widower, a fifty-seven-year-old farmer whose daughter, Della, had married Peter's oldest son a few years earlier. When the two men returned Peter, who'd told the press about countless other trips, let Forsythe do the talking.

*"We saw all kinds of statuary in Europe, some good and some bad," said H.K. 'Doc' Forsythe who, along with Peter Hopley, returned yesterday from a trip across the water. "I am here to tell you that when we steamed into New York harbor and saw the Goddess of Liberty looming up in the foreground, she looked mighty good to me."*

*Mr. Forsythe spent half an hour in this office describing the trip he took with Peter Hopley. (Atlantic News Telegraph, September 14, 1914.)*

Forsythe's first and only trip abroad was an adventure he would not soon forget. They traveled across in style—because of turmoil in Europe few civilians were headed that way—and set off to buy horses. They traveled mostly by train and coach until reaching Ireland. There Hopley called on an acquaintance he'd met on previous trips and borrowed an automobile.  They traveled, it would seem, as much for pleasure as business.  One evening they learned that legal provisions had been enacted allowing for the confiscation of automobiles to be used in the war effort.  This sent them scurrying.  Forsythe was quoted as saying that, although they were 200 miles away from the home of the car's owner and the roads were bad, they made the journey in just one day.  The article fails to tell us who drove.  Peter seems to have been enthusiastic about automobiles, but once told a reporter he'd absolutely never get into an airplane.

Hopley found a few horses and agreed on price.  Because of the accelerating strife there were extensive procedures to be complied with in order to get horses out of the country.  The process was a snarl at best, and likely not to succeed at all.  The arrangement Hopley reached had the seller assuming responsibility for transportation.  Forsythe told the reporter that Hopley would not pay until shipment was guaranteed.  This was wise, as the war spread and intensified and the horses almost certainly never left Europe.

In later years it was said that Hopley and Forsythe were overseas when the war broke out.  This was probably not precisely the case.  The generally accepted start of the war, the first battle of the Marne, began on September 4.  The two were at sea when that happened.  They were certainly in Europe, however, at a dangerous and historic time.

The trip home was not nearly as pleasant as the one going.  Americans were fleeing in droves; every ship was packed.  Hopley's advance booking meant nothing.  He and Forsythe took what they could get—cots in a crowded room far below deck in what was called steerage—quarters that were the most primitive and, under ordinary circumstances, the least expensive.  They paid dearly to share cramped compartments with, Forsythe said, others who were accustomed to better accommodations.  These included two opera singers, some actors, and several businessmen Forsythe thought to be worth millions.

Hopley, who had made the trip dozens of times, was accustomed to fine dining during passage.  He apparently felt, even under the circumstances, that a man with money in his purse could purchase food.  He took aboard only a couple of bananas to hold him over until the steamer got under way and regular meals were served.  There were, according to Forsythe, no regular meals. As he was inexperienced and more cautious, he heeded advice to pack multiple lunches. The Forsythe trunk was well stocked. Peter Hopley did not dine in the manner in which he was accustomed, but thanks to Doc Forsythe neither did he go hungry.

The Telegraph looked up Hopley a couple of days later to get his comments on the journey. Hopley was not interested in discussing details of travel, or even the horses he may or may not have acquired. He guided the interview to the hostilities in Europe. What had started as an isolated act of violence, not expected to have an impact on world affairs, was rapidly developing into a full-blown war.

Hopley, while abroad that summer of 1914, read the newspapers, talked to people. He did not, due to hostilities, enter Germany. He usually did so, being on friendly terms with T.R. Wallace, who was the American consul in the German city of Crefoldt.

Crefoldt, also known as Krefeld, is a city near the Rhine in western Germany. In addition to Wallace, Hopley had German acquaintances there from whom he'd bought Percheron stallions. He was speaking with a measure of insight when he told the Telegraph he believed prospects in Europe were grim. The military might of Germany and allies were, he feared, too much for England and France. At the time the U.S. was maintaining neutrality. President Wilson vowed repeatedly that our nation would not become involved, and Hopley took him at his word. He believed that, without American intervention, Germany would soon control Europe.

Germany did not, largely because Wilson changed his position. Thousands of American boys answered the call in 1917. Among them was Peter's youngest son, Wayland.

*Beulah, Margaret and Eda taken shortly before Beulah's death in 1895*

*Beulah and Margaret in 1882*

*Francis Arrowsmith Hopley, about 1885*

*Edith*

*Edna in 1910*

*Edna with Minnie and Mary*

*Harry Hopley ready to judge a livestock show*

*Harry Hopley two or three years before his death*

*Hopley mansion in Lewis.*
*Edna hired a chauffeur for the "driving season"*

*Another view of the Hopley home*

*Edna's hydrangea and other plants*

*Originally built as a holding place for livestock shipments between the farm and depot, Peter Hopley made this a livery and "stallion barn" when Hopley Switch was built*

*Hopley's livery with car, horses, and buggy*

*Peter with his daily transportation for short trips. This rig, or one similar to it, took him backward over the bank of the East Nishnabotna*

*Peter as he looked after returning from the west*

*House in Lewis in 1910*

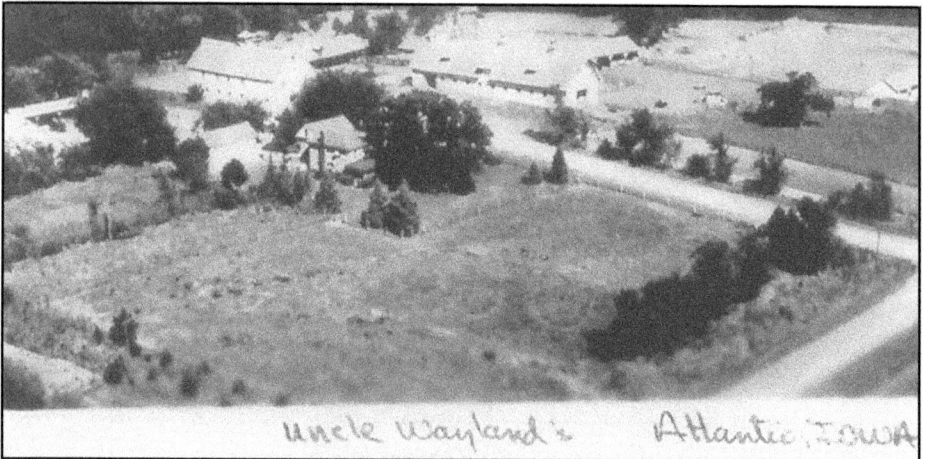

*Aerial photo of West Side Farm after Harry's death
and sale to Wayland*

*Peter and Edna in travel status shortly before her death*

*Minnie, who was called "Hop," at age 18*

*Peter in about 1915*

*The twins in 1902*

*The Hopley children in 1890. Harry is about eight years old*

*Margaret, Edna, Mary and Minnie*

*Peter, in his 70s, put on weight but continued to ride spirited horses*
**Photographs courtesy of Richard Muffley,
from his grandmother's collection.**

# Chapter Thirteen

Wayland, born on the farm in 1895, graduated from Lewis high school in 1912. He studied animal husbandry at Iowa State University, then transferred to the University of Iowa. The latter had a reputation as a school where there was a lot of partying going on, and Wayland was not burdened by the need to work for his tuition. A member of Delta Chi fraternity, he had his share of good times. While a student at the U. of Iowa he met Helen Haw.

Helen Haw was the daughter of George and Genevieve Lauder Haw, part of a well-to-do Ottumwa family. She graduated the same year as Wayland. Helen had an interest in history and genealogy, traced hers to the Revolutionary War, and became a member of the D.A.R. She was an attractive and articulate young woman, dressed well, carried an aura of culture and refinement. She could also, a former Cass County sheriff would later attest, swear like a sailor. If she didn't pick this up from Wayland, he at least expanded her vocabulary.

Helen and Edna are said to have gotten along well, although they knew each other only briefly.

Wayland and Helen were married just prior to his departure for France (twenty-five years later their oldest son, George, would be married shortly before his division shipped for Europe.) Wayland was assigned to the an animal transportation unit, his duty primarily to help care for the thousands of army horses that were, sadly, being shelled and gassed along with men. Peter no doubt had mixed feelings about his youngest son going to war. He had some familiarity with the German military, followed the news from Europe closely, and knew American boys by the thousands were destined to be killed or terribly injured. On the other hand he knew, as Wayland made preparations to leave, that France was occupied by German forces, was on the verge of collapse, after which Hopley's beloved England seemed sure to fall.

Peter might have drawn an interesting comparison—at an age when he was tending horses and fighting Indians in Wyoming and Colorado, his son would be tending horses and fighting Germans in France.

It was not, however, Peter Hopley's thoughts on the war that garnered him the most publicity during those years. His article on how he became a millionaire was published and widely reprinted during 1918. He stressed hard work, thrift and saving, followed by calculated risks and rewards, all rungs on the ladder of Capitalism, and newspaper editors far from Cass County, Iowa, took notice. Some credited the source. Others avoided copyright issues by rewording his statements. The First National Bank in Stevens Point, Wisconsin, was one of the banks that felt his story might attract depositors and printed a paid advertisement, telling how a southwest Iowa farmer (unnamed) had worked and saved and made a fortune.

The war officially ended in November, 1918. Some American soldiers would not return home for several months. Wayland Hopley, who had gone through the war without a reportable injury, was still in France when he received word that both his mother and a sister were dead.

The headline in the News Telegraph on February 15, 1919, told the story.

*Shock Caused by Daughter's Death Kills Mrs. Hopley*
*Deaths an Hour Apart*
*Mrs. Peter Hopley died last night at the home of her daughter, Mrs. Edna Askew of Valley Junction, at the news of her daughter's death an hour earlier. Mrs. Hopley's death came without a moment's warning. Mrs. Askew's death came at the Methodist Hospital in Des Moines at 10:30 last night. The mother's death took place an hour later.*

*With Mrs. Hopley when she died were her daughters, Mrs. F.W. (Margaret) Lumsden and Mrs. Clarence (Edith) Hedges. They had just returned from the hospital where their sister had died. They went to the bedroom where their mother had retired to tell her of the death of their sister, Edna. When Mrs. Hopley heard the news she collapsed and died almost immediately.*

*Mrs. Hopley had been in poor health for six months past. Among other ailments she had high blood pressure. Recently she was at Colfax, going to Valley Junction a few days ago to be with her daughter. Her husband and her son, Harry, were also at Valley Junction.*

*Mrs. Askew had been ill since Jan. 1. Last Monday she submitted to an operation, from which she failed to rally.*

*Mrs. Hopley was 64 years of age. She was born on the farm of her father, Leonard Everly, which is now a part of the Hopley ranch north of Lewis. She was married to Mr. Hopley in 1874. Beside her husband, she is survived by five children. They are Mrs. Fred Muffley of Fairfield, Idaho; Mrs. F.W. Lumsden of Storm Lake, Mrs. Clarence Hedges of Garden Grove, Ia,; Harry of Lewis and Wayland, who is now in France.*

*Mrs. Hopley was one of the best known women in Cass County and was known by a wide circle of friends. The Hopley home has been in Lewis for several years.*

The article included details concerning the Askew family, one of which was that Edna Hopley Askew had a nine-year old son (Peter Askew, named for his grandfather. A portion of Peter Hopley's estate was to eventually go to Edna or her descendant. Young Peter Askew's share would not be paid until years after it should have been).

The paper concluded this item with details of Edna's lengthy illness, saying she had, on at least one occasion, accompanied her mother to Colfax for mineral spa treatments.

A double funeral followed.

From the front page of February 17, 1919:

*Mrs. Hopley and Daughter Buried*
*Largest Funeral in the History of Lewis*
*Funeral services were held at the Congregational Church in Lewis at one o'clock for Mrs. Peter Hopley and her daughter, Mrs. E.J. Askew, whose deaths occurred an hour apart on Friday night. No funeral services in Lewis were ever larger attended than those today. The services were conducted by the Rev. B.F. Myers of Oakland, formerly pastor of the Congregational church here and to which Mrs. Hopley and her daughter were members.*

*The church was crowded, many being present from out of town. There were a great many present from Atlantic.*

*The remains of Mrs. Hopley and her daughter arrived in Lewis at noon and were taken directly to the church. Burial was in the Lewis cemetery.*

Another article appeared elsewhere on the front page:
*The bodies of Mrs. Hopley and her daughter arrived in Atlantic yesterday evening from Valley Junction. The former's death occurred an hour after that of her daughter at a hospital in Des Moines. The bodies were accompanied by immediate members of the Hopley and Askew families. The funeral parties left on the Rock Island for Lewis at 11:30 am today.*

*A short funeral service was held in Des Moines yesterday afternoon at the Dunn Funeral Home.*

In the years following his wife's death, Peter relinquished more farming responsibility to his sons. He spent his winters in California, Arizona, Florida. He either gave or sold his vineyard to Margaret and her husband, who moved there shortly after Peter died.

In late February of 1926, in what the paper called a journey to "look into his extensive holdings," Hopley left again for the west coast. The trip was to be an extended one. He planned to spend time with the Harris family and other friends, with people who tended crops and grape vines on land he owned, probably take a train ride and spend a few days—or weeks—in San Diego. When he arrived he was said to be in good spirits and health. Shortly thereafter he contracted pneumonia. He died in a Los Angeles hospital on March 18 at the age of seventy-nine.

Funeral services for his wife and daughters were held in the Congregational Church. For his own service he had chosen his home.

On a raw, unpleasant afternoon in mid-March the main floor of the Hopley mansion filled with relatives, neighbors, livestock producers, politicians and, of course, local newspaper representatives. Most attendees found a seat. Latecomers stood in the entry. A few men, overcoat collars up-turned, stood on the porch. They heard the story, which most had heard often, of the original trip from England, of horses, cattle, success. Hopley was referred to at the service, and in his obituary, as *"one of the best-known men in the Midwest."* His brother, William, had rated only *"one of the best known men in the county."*

The funeral was the last Hopley family event held in the mansion. Peter and Edna's children and grandchildren followed his casket from the house and never returned.

At the cemetery, graveside services were conducted by members of Atlantic's Elks Lodge.

Charles Chase, editor and publisher of the Telegraph, felt more than an obituary (of which his paper had an extensive one) was in order. He wrote the following for his editorial page:

*One by one the men who pioneered this country and laid the foundations for the matchless commonwealth it has become are passing on. Time is relentless and those pioneers who have not already answered the summons are in the twilight of life. It is something worthwhile to have lived in one community for half a century or more and been a part of its very development, to have contributed to every spiritual and material advancement the years have wrought. To have seen the wilderness subdued and the prairies blossom like a rose; to have endured the privations of the early beginnings and to have moved on and up as the years brought their change in standards of living; to have been a part of all of it constitutes a romance of living only those who were in and of have known.*

*About the time that Peter Hopley came to this country a United States senator was insisting on the floor of the US Senate that the western part of Iowa will never be inhabited to any considerable extent; that it would remain a hunting grounds for Indians; and that if he were asked to fix the western boundaries of Iowa he would place them between Des Moines and Adair. That he was sincere in this belief no one will question, but that he lacked the vision others had which peopled this section with God-fearing and God-loving people, built its towns and cities and converted its virgin prairies into farms than which there are none better in the world, has been demonstrated again and again.*

*Peter Hopley, whose funeral was held this afternoon at the Hopley home in Lewis and whose remains have been committed to the earth he loved, had faith in this section half a hundred years ago and that faith he never lost. The Hopley estate between this city and Lewis consisting of more than 2,000 acres of land and innumerable buildings is the best evidence of the faith he held and which he passed on to his sons and daughters. He has left a matchless heritage. To him and all his kind, who endured and labored as he did, a debt of gratitude will be forever due. They that built better than they knew will not be questioned.*

*On the day before Peter Hopley left for California where he died, he called at this office and he and this writer visited together for an hour or more. It was the best visit they ever had and this writer treasures it beyond the power of expression. Together we relived the years we had known each other, the many outstanding events which emphasized our times, and together recalled the many they had known who have laid down their burdens and gone on to the silent majority. There was no indication that they would not meet again. There was discussion of spending next winter in Florida.*

*A dedicated citizen, a devoted husband, a loving father, and staunch friend, he will live long in the memory of those who knew him.*

Harry, then forty-five years of age, had purchased several hundred acres in partnership with his father. Wayland, who was thirty-two when his father died, was living in the home he built for Helen near the site of Peter and Edna's original farm house. The brothers were jointly farming more than 2,000 acres, plus overseeing a cow-calf operation on several hundred acres in Nebraska. Their nearby cousins, the offspring of William and Mary Okell Hopley, had 1,000 acres themselves. The family, both branches, owned scores of horses, many quite valuable, along with hundreds of purebred cattle and hogs. There were crops in the bins and hay in the barns.

Up the road the William Hopley place was managed by Thomas who, as has been noted, never married. He did not, however, live alone. He resided for his entire lifetime in a small part of the big, two story home his father had built for a family that included seven children. His sister, Jennie, four years his senior, stayed on for a couple of years after William died. When she moved to Atlantic the youngest sibling, Mabel, did the housekeeping.

Frank achieved adulthood with no room for him on the farm. After marrying Elizabeth Spencer of Hamlin in 1902 they rented a farm in Audubon County. In 1908, the year his father died, he bought a farm in South Dakota where they would live for twenty-three years. Between 1910 and 1914 three daughters were born. After six childless years, Elizabeth delivered a son. He was named after Frank's older brother or, more likely, their grandfather.

Thomas, particularly in the years just prior to and following William's death, bought and sold a lot of land. He bought land in Marne, traded a 120 farm in Cass County for 600 acres in Keith County, Nebraska. This trade was later negated, through no fault of Thomas'. The Nebraska land was part of an estate. The man trading it may have thought he had the authority to do so, but did not. Thomas disposed of his 120 acres in another manner.

On one date alone—March 3, 1908—Thomas Hopley's name was published in association with three real estate transfers. He made several other deals in 1908 and 1909. In 1910 he bought a half-section in California. He was also named in several lawsuits. None of these were as sensational as brother John managed, but were troublesome. The bank of Adair took him to court over a $100 note. An earlier article tells us the case of Conway and Case, implement dealers, vs. Thomas Hopley was settled out of court.

Thomas, over the years, managed to sell more property than he acquired. Some may have gone to pay medical expenses. Like his father, he developed health problems at an early age. Heart trouble was the worst of it, although pneumonia was listed as the cause of death when he passed in 1931. He, like several others in the family, was cared for in his final days by his sister, Sophia, in the home at 611 Poplar Street she shared with her husband, Dr. C.L. Campbell.

When Thomas died in 1931 Frank and Elizabeth sold out in South Dakota and moved back to the home place. Their oldest daughter had by then married and remained in South Dakota. The other two girls came to Cass County and later married men from Atlantic.

The door was finally open for Frank, the only son of William Hopley to have a son, to return to his boyhood home. He was fifty-six years of age, his son, Tommy, eleven. The move was one Frank Hopley wanted to make, although the farm was several hundred acres smaller than it had once been, and the Great Depression was just setting in. There wasn't a lot Frank could do but hold things together, to be the custodian, wait for better times, and groom his son to one day build on what there was.

Because Frank and his older brother were not close, Tommy Hopley may have met his cousin George for the first time at Thomas's funeral. George, Wayland's oldest son, was then ten.

Wayland and Helen Haw Hopley had two other sons, Wayland, Jr. (called Hickory), born in 1924, and Peter (Pete) who was born in 1931, just a few days after Thomas died. They expected there'd be a place for them if they wanted it, but George was the oldest, the one who would take over.

These were the boys—George, the oldest grandson of Peter Hopley, and Tommy, the only son of a son of William Hopley—who were the heirs apparent. Both would come of age near the outbreak of World War ll.

# Chapter Fourteen

Throughout their brief lives George and Tommy Hopley had countless occasions to view, and probably climb over, one of the most unusual fences in the area. They probably didn't see it as such, having grown up with lengthy rows of concrete posts being part of the landscape. The fence was there when George was born, there when Tommy moved with his family to Cass County, there when the two boys were taken to the Atlantic depot on their way to war. Others, however, saw the fence for the first time and wondered why anyone would go to the work and expense of two solid miles of concrete fence posts. A family that made the news for lesser achievements erected a fence that attracted the attention of at least three newspapers.

Harry, three years before his mother died, ten before his father passed, began work on an edifice that both served a purpose and stood as a reminder of Hopley farms long after Hopley farms had ceased to be.

Men of Peter's generation said of the hedge apple tree, also called the Osage orange, that fence posts made of it would last for fifty years, after which they could be dug up, turned on end, re-set, and re-used for another fifty. Only the portion above ground, exposed to animals and weather, would show wear. And who, old timers asked, needed a fence post that would last more than 100 years?

Apparently Harry Hopley. The following appeared in the Telegraph in May of 1916:

*Pearl and George Keffer of Lewis are putting in two miles of woven wire fence for Harry Hopley on the White Pole Road.*

*The fence is of cement posts and woven wire.  The corner posts are 8 foot high.  It will be the best fence in Cass County when done.*

The Lewis paper did a story before the fence was finished, as did the Griswold American.

The Keffers were life-long residents of Lewis, parents of Viola, Bernard (town marshal for many years) Bernice, and Ronnie. George Keffer is remembered as being a brick mason and cement worker.

In January of 1916, with the war escalating in Europe, the U.S. remaining neutral, Peter and Edna (he was then sixty-nine, she was sixty-one) took a trip to Hawaii.  While they were gone Harry, who by then had become the decision-maker, held a special hog sale in the pavilion at the Cass County fairgrounds.  The sale bill boasted that Hopley's Hampshires were the finest to be had, in part because they *"fattened on less grain than other breeds."*  *"They are the best grass hogs,"* the sale bill promised, and a follow-up article says there were plenty of anxious buyers.

With his father relaxing on a beach in Hawaii, Harry went to the National Livestock Show in Denver, where he purchased the grand champion load of feeder calves.  The calves sold for what news accounts say was then a record price; $14.50 per hundred.  All were Aberdeen Angus.  These were perhaps not the first Angus cattle on the Hopley farm, but they're the first we can confirm.  Harry liked his Herfords and Shorthorns, and didn't forsake them.  At the same auction he bought a carload of the latter.

Harry got the Keffers started on the fence, then shipped ten choice registered Shorthorn heifers to a buyer in California.  He also put his father on a train for the Mayo Clinic.  Peter, suffering from gallstones, had not enjoyed Hawaii as much as he otherwise might have.

As the summer of 1916 passed the Keffers made steady progress on the fence, a job that took several months.  The "best fence in Cass County," as the paper called it, would require over 700 posts.  Digging the holes, making forms, hand-mixing and pouring concrete took time, particularly for corner posts.  News article pointed out their height, eight feet, but the reinforced posts actually extended an additional four feet into the ground. Concrete corner bracing was poured horizontally in two directions, creating massive structures from which woven and barbed wire could be stretched as tightly as desired. Harry had once been named in a lawsuit when a cow went through a fence and was struck by a car. This fence, he expected, would contain anything the family cared to keep.

A few of the posts remain nearly a century later. Spaced at sixteen foot intervals, some are still in use. The tops of corner posts, probably struck by lightning on more than one occasion, have been whittled to less than their original height. Rebar protrudes, time and weather have worn down concrete, but the corner posts, with eyebolts put in place by the Keffers in 1916, made this a fence that was "horse high, bull strong, and hog tight."

With Peter in Rochester, Harry then made what the papers construed to be an important business deal with a "*Mr. Brown, head cattle man for Armor Packing Company.*" Brown was in Atlantic for the purpose of making a long-term arrangement having to do with Hopley hogs.

Harry Hopley obviously knew his livestock and had a good head for business. He was also in remarkable physical condition. When he returned from Knox College at the age of twenty-two, where he'd starred in football, he signed on to play with Atlantic's semi-pro team, The Maroons. (Harry actually started school at Iowa State, where he studied agriculture. We can speculate that he went to Knox, a smaller school located in Galesburg, Illinois, because his chances of playing football were better there. Another possibility has to do with the origins of the school, which was founded in the 1830s by a group of anti-slavery social reformers. The Reverend Samuel Wright, one of the more outspoken originators of Knox, was openly supportive of the Underground Railroad. Knox was the site of the fifth Lincoln-Douglas debate. This would have endeared the place to Harry's grandfather. He'd been dead, though, for ten years when Harry was born, so football seems a more likely lure than politics.)

Semi-professional football teams such as the Maroons were "professional" only in the most marginal manner. Admission was charged to their contests, which was divided among players. The pot, though, often did not cover travel expense. Opponents ranged from other small-town teams to those representing big-city breweries and packing plants. Some, including Hopley, played both baseball and football. Schedules were haphazard, officials not necessarily competent. Fans were rowdy, sometimes drunk, rarely the best of sports. Baseball games of the time frequently erupted into brawls. Football, violent when played by the rules, could boil over into fracases even more brutal.

Harry Hopley was still playing at the age of thirty-five.

The game has changed much since 1916. So has the protective gear. The sport was, and is, a young man's game. To be knocking heads while wearing a skinny leather helmet and little else for padding, against muscular men ten years younger, was not for the faint of heart. Hopley not only did it, he excelled.

*November 16, 1916. The Atlantic Maroons defeated the Dunlap Giants, 23-6. Franklin opened the scoring with a touchdown in the first quarter, Hopley kicking the goal. The Maroons then held, and Hopley received. He ran 105 yards to the score, then kicked the goal against a strong wind. (Atlantic Telegraph)*

The article goes on to tell us that Harry Hopley, in addition to playing running back, kicking field goals (he hit a 35-yarder in that game), and punting, also starred on defense. His Maroons, another article reported, *"had gone an incredible six years without giving up a point"* (this was either an error on the reporter's part, a typo, or a "point" meant something else at the time. The Maroons, only days before, had been scored on during their win over Dunlap).

A week and a half after the Dunlap game, Harry shipped three more rail cars of Shorthorn and Hereford bulls to California. The buyers, it was written, had looked at stock on several Midwest farms, then opted to make their entire purchase from Hopley.

On the 17th of February, 1917, headlines were devoted to the sinking of an Italian troop ship. Only two of those on board survived. A liner from Holland went to the bottom under suspicious circumstances. German U-boats were prowling shipping lanes, and the United States was edging closer to war.

Harry had yet another stock sale that month, a bit of an unusual one as he offered the full gamut—purebred horses, cattle, and hogs. Horses alone brought over $12,000, with an exceptional Shire mare bringing the top individual price of $500. One of Harry's prized shorthorn bulls went for $400.

Wayland, his brother's junior by nearly fifteen years, came home from the University of Iowa in the early summer of 1917. It would, for him, be a particularly eventful season. He had proposed marriage to Helen Haw and she'd accepted. In early June the couple approved a set of plans and work got underway on yet another fine home; this one on Peter's Riverside Farm.

This country's entry into the war brought a curious set of circumstances for the family. Harry, thirty-six and therefore exempt from the draft, was selected to serve on the Cass County Draft Exemption board. In that position he would have a voice, and a vote, on those petitions filed by men who received induction orders but felt, for whatever reason, they should not be called. Wayland Hopley, about to be married and take his place in Cass County's biggest farm operation, received his draft notice.

There is no way of knowing what might have happened. Farming was a vital function, producing the food and material armies must have. Exceptions were given for less. Peter Hopley was a powerful man, Harry an influential one and in a place to do his brother—and family—a favor. Iowa, according to a news article, led the nation in exemption requests—largely because so much of the population was engaged in agriculture. Had Wayland sought to avoid the draft, he might also have asked a favor of Dr. Campbell, who was named physician on the county draft board. Dr. Campbell performed the physicals.

Wayland Hopley didn't ask, nor did a lot of other boys from Lewis. Frank and Ray Enfield, brothers who grew up there, enlisted then died of disease. Jess Smiley was gassed, but recovered. Guy Peters, also of Lewis, was struck in the chest by an explosive round during the final days of the war and died a few hours later. Altogether more than seventy young men with a Lewis address were either drafted or enlisted.

In early July Hopley family members traveled to Ottumwa, where Wayland married Helen Haw. Peter and Edna watched the marriage of their youngest, then returned to Lewis. They may have traveled to

Ottumwa by auto rather than train, as shortly after their return Peter sold his Aero (the second one he'd had) and bought a new one. He also purchased a new Ford truck.

Edna could adapt to modern conveniences. So did Peter.

While Peter was getting used to his new Ford, the newlyweds took a short trip to Colorado. Their home was being built, but months away from completion. Wayland returned, took his induction physical, Dr. Campbell passed him, and he was soon in a training camp in Battle Creek, Michigan. Peter visited him there in September. Edna, perhaps not feeling well, apparently didn't go.

Wayland was commissioned, made first lieutenant and assigned to the 303rd Advance Animal Transport Depot. During the year of 1917 he was a college student, a bridegroom and honeymooner, a draftee and, before the year was out, on board a ship bound for France.

Edna seems to have been relatively healthy by that Christmas season, Peter fully recovered from his gallstone operation. Harry and Della, married then eight years, still had no children. They had, however, taken into their home, and were raising, a niece of Della's named Eleanor Forsyth.

Harry and Della would never be as socially active as Edna and Peter. When Peter traveled he did so with company, took side trips, saw the sights, took his time. He climbed the Eiffel Tower, drove the back roads of Scotland, made friends and socialized on trip after trip.

Harry's travels were, at least on the surface, more focused on business. He had no children of his own to take along. There was Eleanor, but she was closer to Della and if Della stayed behind, which she usually did, so did Eleanor.

With the passage of time Harry's reputation as a judge and breeder of livestock grew. He added to that reputation by being at major stock shows, either demonstrating, buying, selling, and responding to requests for advice. He went, he judged, he bought and sold, and then returned home. He most often went alone. It was said that he liked to play cards, and may have enjoyed a game of poker.

Della had her friends. She was active in the Lewis Crescent Club. In early 1918 she hosted fifty past and current members of that club to what the paper called a "scrumptious lunch." We do not, however, often find her at the gala balls of the late 19-teens and twenties. She was social, but didn't make the papers the way her mother-in-law did.

Harry, with Christmas approaching, with his younger brother in France waiting for the spring offensive, made a purchase that was a signal of things to come. The Lewis Standard, in an article printed on Christmas Eve of 1917, reported that *"Harry Hopley has purchased, from P.H. Pettinger of Cumberland, a Titan tractor, which he will use on the Hopley Farms."*

The Titan was little more than an iron frame with a gasoline tank and engine resting on steel wheels. It could be driven down the road and taken to the field, but had very little traction, was difficult to steer, was helpless in mud and prone to mire even in soft soil. The tractor had a flywheel. Hopley's purchase was largely an experiment, the flywheel used to run a belt-driven grinder and corn sheller. The horse barns remained, as did the big animals. Harry liked his horses, and converting to the internal combustion engine for farm use took time. Machinery designed for horses could be modified in some cases, not in others. The same was true of men.

An example of this was described in a newspaper published in a town not far from Lewis. It told, in a series of random articles extending from 1917 until the 1940s, the story of Harry Rae. Rae was man of about the same age as Harry Hopley, had much in common with him and the Hopley farm hands. While Rae wasn't a semi-pro football player, as a young man he was in good shape; a champion corn-husker had to be. The contests Rae entered amounted to a man, a team, a wagon, and judges with stop watches. The standard contest had each competitor picking for one hour, after which the amount picked was weighed, deductions made for any ear that was unpicked or missed the wagon. The sport, if we can call it that, doesn't sound either difficult or grueling. It was. Neither basketball nor football; certainly not baseball, requires non-stop motion for an hour. There were no huddles, no time-outs. Anyone of average physical ability could pick corn. Not many could do so on a par with Harry Rae. Pick an ear, snap the husk, toss it toward the wagon without looking, the next ear being picked and launched before the previous one landed. The horses needed to know their role, which was to keep the wagon where the picker needed it to be. Rae was a regular in annual corn picking contests, and he almost always placed high. One year he went to the state finals.

His horses, which he prided himself on, were trained to as near to perfection as was possible. He preferred to work his plowing teams in a span, eight horses wide, saying he got more horsepower that way. *"They don't pull as hard,"* Harry was quoted, *"when they're two by two. Only the lead horses can see what's ahead. The others have a view that doesn't encourage work."*

Turning horses in an eight-wide span pulling a heavy plow or disc is a touchy task. The one to the inside moves slowly, marking time, the one outside more briskly, those between holding the line. Turning too short results in a tangle, too wide in a missed row. A local newsman made it a point to watch while Harry worked his eight-horse team. With sixteen reins in his hands, a feel for each of them, *"he could turn that span on a dime,"* the reporter wrote, *"and have enough change left over for a cup of coffee."*

Rae, with the coming of the tractor, did not do well. He lost his job as a farm manager and took one as a hired hand. Tractors frustrated him. He did not understand them. He could work with a horse, communicate, teach it do his bidding. He could not train a tractor. He began drinking heavily. In the late 1930s, driving a tractor pulling a two–bottom plow, he came to the end of a row and couldn't remember how to turn. In his confusion he forgot how to apply the brake. He ripped out a section of fence and plowed a thirty-foot-long furrow across a dirt road before he got the machine to whoa. Rumor had it he was drunk. There was no questioning his condition when, a few years later, he had a similar problem while pulling a corn planter. The planter had been made for horses so it was necessary for someone to be on it, pulling levers that would raise and lower the planting blades. The rider either fell or jumped clear when Harry drove through a fence. He watched as Harry, pulling back on the steering wheel, yelling 'whoa,' started up a steep road bank. Halfway up the tractor's front end came off the ground. Harry, leaning back on the reins and shouting commands as the front wheels rose to the tipping point, was crushed and died at the scene.

It would be interesting to know what Wayland Hopley thought when mail call came and he received a letter telling of Harry's purchase of a tractor. He was, at the time, in the midst of a small army of horses. The folly of cavalry charges had, by then, ceased. The slaughter of horses had not.

# Chapter Fifteen

If Wayland Hopley was a sentimental man, he concealed it well. People remember him as gruff, hard-talking, profane. His father was forty-seven, and away from home a great deal, when Wayland was born. Harry was probably as much a father figure as Peter. Both Peter and Harry were knowledgeable horsemen. In Wayland's youth they built as fine a horse barn as there was to be found. A newspaper article depicts one of their barns as being 122 feet long, 68 feet wide with a full loft and an attached 38'x24' el, a "loafing shed" where animals might be harnessed and unharnessed, held for a time between the field and the stable.

A full-length center aisle was bordered on each side by rows of stalls and mangers interrupted by intermittent grain bins. There were also sleeping quarters where seasonal workers could bunk. The mow overhead, before hay balers were used, was packed each summer with red clover and grass, providing both fodder and insulation. With two Hopley farms, one on the west side of the river, another on the east, one horse barn wasn't enough. A second was erected, then a third. All were immaculately kept; stalls cleaned daily, a fresh coat of paint when needed. As time passed the painted words across the barns changed. We find photographs of them with the words "Riverside Farm," "Peter Hopley's Imported Horses," "West Side Farm," "Hopley Farm," "Hopley and Son," "Hopley and Sons" and eventually, in the 1950s, "Hopley Stock Farm." The letters were never allowed to fade.

Wayland grew up with horses. Men of that era tended not to form long-term attachments to their animals. Working horses were comparable to vehicles today—we have our favorites, the best car ever, the finest tractor a man could own—but when the time comes to trade we're content with fond memories. Peter loved his Suffolk Punches, but he probably never owned one he wouldn't sell. Harry Rae, who turned to drink and erratic behavior when he had little choice but to farm with tractors, never loved a horse to the extent he couldn't part with it. He once raised a colt he particularly liked, spent months training what many thought was as good a saddle horse as was to be found in southwest Iowa. He sold it to a buyer representing the DuPont family, bid the animal farewell, and set about training another.

Even though sentiment toward horses was limited, they were not machines. Wayland was in a position to see and deal with heart-wrenching situations. There are numerous accounts, including photographs, depicting the carnage wrought upon both man and beast during our First World War. Horses and mules did not wear helmets. They were not equipped with gas masks. They did not ordinarily share the protection of the trenches. They were vital to the war effort for both sides. While there are touching accounts of dazed, sometimes wounded animals wandering into no-man's land while armies of both sides held their fire, more often they were cut down. Artillery deliberately fired long. Killing horses was part of disrupting supply lines. Deadly though weapons of war were, history tells us more horses, driven beyond endurance, died from fatigue than external injuries.

Great Britain, early on, called up 140,000 Shires, Suffolk, Percheron and coach horses. Most stables made an effort to hold back foundation breeding stock. Some were successful, but only for a while. A war that was essentially a one-year, albeit bloody, experience for the United States was four times as long in Europe. As the war drug on more and more horses, blooded stallions and brood mares, were pressed into service. Hopley's unit included veterinarians, as well as officers such as himself who had experience and some formal training in animal care. They could treat the sickness, harness sores, foot rot, mange, malnutrition and dehydration, doing so under pressure to get the animals back on the line. If the injury was severe, would require prolonged time and care, the animal was destroyed.  An estimated 1,000,000 horses and mules were pressed into service.  Several published histories of the war say that one fourth to one half did not survive.

When the war ended in France in November of 1918, another horse slaughter followed.  Shipping them home presented an expensive and logistically difficult proposition, and there were German prisoners to feed.  Thousands of horses were killed and butchered and fed to POWs.

When Harry Hopley said, in 1914, that it would take at least twenty years for the horse breeding program to recover, he was several years short.  By then the tractor was no longer an experiment.  Harry, though, loved his Belgians and as long as he was part of Hopley farms they would be as well.

Harry Hopley, the year the war ended, was elected president of the Iowa Shorthorn Association.  His animals were becoming better-known, their bloodlines performing well.  In May of 1918 he had another Shorthorn sale.  The top-selling bull brought $4,400; ten times as much as the highest price paid for a Hopley shorthorn at the sale a year before.  He shipped seven rail carloads of fat cattle that summer alone, with more going out in the fall and early winter.  Fat lambs, another full rail car, went to market in November.  It was said that grass never grew in corrals at the Hopley Switch.

Joseph's son, Cecil, apparently either ill or otherwise in need of cash, sold some of what had been his father's land.  There wasn't much to sell.  Of the Hopley brothers who came to Iowa in the 1850s, only the farms founded by Peter and William flourished.  William's, by the time of the war, was smaller than it had been.

In October, Harry, who apparently wasn't interested in the land his cousin offered, went to a major stock show in Chicago.  He'd imported a Shorthorn bull named "Village Beau." "Village Clipper," "Village Lad," and a list of bulls with the word "Village" in their names followed.  One of these bulls won best of show at the national competition, all but assuring Hopley that yearling sires from the "Village" line would bring top price.

When he returned home his mother was not well.  Neither was his sister, Edna.  Edna had sought her usual remedy in Colfax, persuading her daughter to do so as well. Apparently both had previously found some relief in the mineral spas, but not this time.

For Edna (the daughter) Surgery in a Des Moines hospital followed, as did her death and that of her mother. Harry was at the house, present with his sisters, when they broke the news that resulted in Edna's collapse.

The double-funeral, which Charles Willey called the biggest Lewis had ever experienced, followed.

Wayland arrived home from France less than two months after his mother and sister were buried. He must have visited Oakwood cemetery, stood among the cedars. The number of stones in the Hopley plot was growing.

Harry celebrated his brother's return by buying $1200 worth of Victory bonds—the federal government's way of borrowing money to pay war debts.

The same federal government was deeply involved in negotiating terms of peace. Germany, seeing serious trouble in governing and rebuilding under the proposed agreement, balked. When they eventually accepted, and they had little choice but to do so, the headlines were the banner on local front pages. The same day there appeared an item announcing that Harry Hopley was leaving as soon as possible for Scotland. He was going to buy more cattle and at least look around for horses. The wheat yield was good that year, the building of another horse and cattle barn got underway, and a few Clydesdales were purchased and brought home from Scotland. Peter made the news by going to the field, a reporter present, and picking a few ears of corn. He was 72 years old.

# Chapter Sixteen

World news in the spring of 1920 continued to be dominated by stories of unrest in Germany. The peace agreement was not good, providing for a government too weak to perform basic functions, to rebuild and unite. German Socialists were angling for an alliance with Russia. The Kapp government resigned under pressure. Allied warships commanded both sides of the Bosphorus. Hitler was lurking, becoming politically active, his ideas forming and his following increasing. Peter, widowed and growing old, told the press he hoped the peace would endure. He, however, would never return to Europe and occupied himself by feeding cattle with Harry and spending his winters in a warmer climate.

In Cass County the news was more about cattle than Hitler. Article after article hailed the area's bourgeoning cattle industry. The impact was noted by other businesses. Sales brought people that filled area hotels, boosted the restaurant trade. Buyers bought more while in town than livestock. In mid-March two large sales were held at the fairgrounds. Stock from the Hopley farm was not offered, but the influence was apparent.

Peter and Harry were in the news when they shipped Shorthorn and Hereford cattle to Nebraska and Colorado and California. While it was selling to out-of-state buyers that made the papers, they were dispersing much more stock locally.

Bloodlines imported by Hopley were celebrated at a gala dinner held at the Hotel Pullman on a March evening following the second major sale of the month. Seventy guests, by invitation only, were present.

Following a dinner that featured elegant appetizers, a soup and salad course, porterhouse steak and various desserts, the speaking began. Matt White, managing editor of *Iowa Homestead* magazine, delivered the keynote address. His journal, which would soon become *Wallace's Farmer,* had carried previous articles written by Peter Hopley. White, in a newspaper interview held later, let it be known that Hopley was welcome to write more.

The president of the Iowa Hereford Cattle association spoke, as did a breeder of Shorthorns. Speeches, including one by the area's most noted auctioneer, Colonel N.G. Kraschel, continued well into the evening. The Colonel spoke at length about prices, predicting the recent upturn would continue for the foreseeable future.

(Nelson G. Kraschel's lived at a time when it was customary for men who had completed auctioneering school to be given the title "Colonel." While Kraschel probably enjoyed the title, he likely preferred being referred to as "governor." His home was Harlan, where he made a living in the teens and twenties farming and auctioneering. During that time Kraschel worked a number of livestock sales in the Atlantic area, including several for the Hopleys. His biography credits him with selling over $50 million in livestock. In the late 1920s he changed his focus to politics. He was elected Lt. Governor in 1932 and, four years later, moved up. He was sworn in as Iowa's governor in January, 1937. Kraschel, a Democrat, was defeated in a bid for re-election.)

One of the featured cattlemen that evening, a heavy seller at the sale, was perhaps a bit into his cups. He was, amidst much good cheer, called upon. He rose to say he thought it best, under the circumstances, if his wife spoke for him. She stood, said she'd done more than enough of that, and there'd be no speech from their quarters.

The Hopley name was not mentioned in articles regarding the banquet. Had Peter been present he'd have likely been asked to speak, or at least noted. He may have had another commitment, not felt well, or had some other reason for passing up the event. Perhaps it was just preferred, this time, to let the light shine on others.

Harry and Wayland could not have attended. Harry had not yet returned from his first post-war trip abroad. Wayland was on his way to New York to meet the shipment. Once the cattle cleared a health inspection, he would take them to a holding facility in New Jersey to be fed and rested in preparation of the train ride to Iowa. Wayland, college educated, married, WWl behind him, settled into a new home with his bride, was assuming his role. The "Son" in Hopley and Son became plural, and the barns were painted once again.

Most of the Shorthorns from that trip were sold in early May. Strong prices held. When the gavel fell to end another Hopley sale at the pavilion, an article says most buyers paid cash and left happy, and the occasion called for another banquet.

Two months after the sale, Harry and Wayland opened the "Hopley Elevator." Located on the farm, near the Hopley rail station, the elevator went into operation a few days before the telephone was installed. An ad told readers the phone line would soon be completed, that the elevator would both buy and sell all types of grain.

Peter made another trip to California that summer. Charles Willey was, as usual, quick to call for an interview.

*Peter Hopley has returned from California after spending considerable time in Imperial Valley, where he added to the land holdings he presently has there. He says the valley is a wonderful "nature's hot house," and the most fruitful spot in the world. Land can be purchased for $125 to $300 per acre and rents for $50 per acre. When asked about the affect of Prohibition on vineyards, Hopley said those vineyards producing wine-making grapes are now making $1,000 per acre, which is more than under the old dispensation, and all are satisfied.*

Hopley went on to talk about irrigation in the Imperial Valley, then volunteered a word about his health. He'd been ill the previous winter (which may have kept him from the Pullman Hotel banquet) but was much improved.

His daughter, Margaret Hopley Lumsden (as her family grew she was called, by both friends and relatives, "Aunt Lum"), was still living in Storm Lake. She and her husband were, in all likelihood, considering moving to California.

Margaret's sister-in-law, Helen Haw Hopley, made the social page that summer by inviting a few guests to her home. The occasion was modest, noteworthy only because it was the first. The gatherings hosted by Helen and Wayland increased as time passed, both in frequency and good cheer.

F.W. Lumsden was known in Cass County primarily because of who his wife was; or, more accurately, who his wife's father was. He probably felt some satisfaction when a story Margaret gave to a Storm Lake newspaper was picked up by the Atlantic News Telegraph.

*F.W. Lumsden, Storm Lake automobile dealer well known as the son-in-law of Peter Hopley of Lewis, was a boyhood friend of Kenesaw Mountain Landis. Lumsedn received a letter a while back from Landis in which the judge expressed his hopes of putting baseball on the high plane it had before the recent scandal.*

Being a childhood friend of Judge Landis, who was then among the most widely-known figures in America and would succeed at rejuvenating the scandal-plagued sport of baseball, was something worth talking about.

Helen's mother made the trip from Ottumwa to spend time with her daughter, particularly during the latter stages of Helen's pregnancy. The baby, born April 7, 1921, was named George Peter. Newspapers took note:

*Wayland Hopley and wife have a son. This is the first grandson on the Hopley side of the family and needless to say Grandpa Peter is walking on air.*

So was Wayland. Harry had no children and never would. It was the younger son who produced the heir-apparent.

A month after George was born the Hopleys had their annual Shorthorn sale at the fairgrounds pavilion. Forty head of top-notch heifers, some bred, including several yearling bulls of the "Village Beau" breeding Harry favored, were offered.

Harry took out ads in several papers, including a half-page, bold letter bill in the Telegraph. The paper returned the favor by printing an article that had been done so often:

*The Hopley Ranch helped put Cass County on the map. No other institution has done more to put Cass County on the map than the Hopley Stock Farm. The home of fine Shorthorns, it is known to every one of the leading breeders. Founded by Peter Hopley, it is now carried on by his sons. . . . "*

And so on. Accompanying the article (the Atlantic paper again referred to the farm as being "south of Atlantic") was a picture taken from a strategic location. A feedlot of fat Shorthorn cattle are at the feed bunk. In the background stands Harry and Della's fine Victorian house, shade trees, and well-kept barns.

The glow resulting from the arrival of baby George was tempered by the results of the annual sale. Total proceeds were $14,000. Top price for a heifer was $650, for a bull, $550. The average price per head was $275.

A year earlier, Harry disclosed, the sale had brought in $107,000, an average per head of $1,800. The 1921 sale had fewer animals, but not that many fewer. The telling number, the worst of news, was the average per animal—down a whopping $1,525 a head.

Shorthorns would eventually be replaced on Hopley Farms, but the breed wasn't the problem. A Hereford sale was held at the pavilion a few days later with similar results. When Col. Kraschel spoke at the Pullman Hotel a few months earlier and said prices would remain strong for the "foreseeable future," he did not define the phrase. Beef was simply on a down cycle, so the Hopley brothers increased their hog population.

Della's social life was largely centered on Crescent Club and bridge. A few weeks after the sale she hosted and served a "dual lunch," to her guests. Peter, still living in the mansion in Lewis, had a picnic at the house. It came on a Saturday afternoon in mid-August, 1921. The affair was a quiet one, casual, nothing comparable to the weddings and events and other receptions Edna had hosted.

Peter had traveled much, but not entertained in the two years since Edna and their daughter died. The birth of a grandson may have prompted the picnic. Whether he was the impetus or not, little George was the center of attention.

The Cass County Classic was an annual livestock show and slate of horse races held at the fairgrounds each September. The event in 1921 drew 600 hogs, 150 cattle, and so many horses *"that it was necessary to make room for them by removing the sheep to another facility."* This report proved premature—sheep men protested and it was the horses that had to be accommodated elsewhere.

An Atlantic resident named Willard Swolley was a long-time regular at the races, but that year his attendance didn't work out.

On the day livestock was brought, prior to the official opening, the mayor and several officers of the Atlantic police conducted a raid on the home Mr. Swolley, which was located near the depot. Swolley, a bootlegger, was charged with violating prohibition laws. He was nailed with a bottle of alcohol (there was likely more hidden that wasn't found) and, in a corn patch near the house, two large barrels of mash.

Although Mr. Swolley was absent, races were well attended. One reporter wrote that several thousand people, during the course of the show, meandered through livestock barns and packed the pavilion while judging was taking place.

During the announcement of winners, three Lewis families were recognized for their contribution in cattle—the Woodwards, the Kennedy Brothers, and the Hopleys. All showed Shorthorns. Quite possibly the Woodward and Kennedy boys got their start with breeding stock imported by Peter and Harry Hopley.

Another fine banquet followed, and another, and Harry Hopley offered some advice and insight into his life at an oyster supper in October. 125 stockmen, their wives, assorted youngsters, and members of the Cass County Boys and Girls Pig Club assembled at the Woodman Hall for a dinner sponsored by the Cass County Pure Bred Livestock Association. Following bowls of oyster soup the tables were cleared for the usual gamut of speakers. All had words of advice and encouragement for young people interested in pursuing farming and stock production.

One of the briefest messages was delivered by Harry Hopley. He spoke not just to the youth, but had a word of advice for adults. Producers, he suggested, should see to it that their sons and daughters be given animals they could call their own. He took it a step further. *"All the boys and girls in the county that want to should have an animal to raise. I know, because the colt my father gave me, and on which I won a prize, was responsible for putting me in the horse breeding business."*

Harry, who is referred to elsewhere as a regular and long-time supporter of the Boys and Girls Pig Club, had an abundance of hogs and gave a few of them to youngsters. Eleanor, the niece he and Della were raising, was among the recipients. She, however, preferred city life and would eventually make her home in Omaha. She eventually inherited Harry and Della's estate, but had no interest in living on the farm.

Articles such as the one above, in which Harry Hopley fondly recalls a colt given him by his father, then asks livestock producers to donate so *"All the boys and girls in the county that want to should have an animal to raise,"* paint the picture of a sensitive and sentimental man. He may have been, but when not in a public setting he was loud and profane. Contemporaries of Harry and Wayland included the Kennedy brothers; Earl, Glen, Lester and Lou. They also raised and showed shorthorn cattle. Lou Kennedy farmed land that adjoined Harry Hopley's place on the west. His son, Bob, was born in 1924. Bob remembers a Harry Hopley who used vulgar language to the extreme. "Wayland was bad, too," Kennedy said, "maybe just as bad." Those we interviewed who knew the Hopleys of that generation, and the one that followed, nearly all remarked on their coarse language. Exceptions were George and Tommy, both said to be soft-spoken and refined.

In the days following the banquet Harry saw to the preparation of several heifers for the National Livestock Stock Show that would be held in November. He also was reminded of the loss of a diamond ring.

A story about the original incident did not, for whatever reason, appear in Cass County papers at the time the robbery took place. We expect Harry was no more anxious to see the account in print than his father had been when he backed a horse and buggy into the East Nishnabotna.

It seems that in the fall of 1920 Harry, while on in Oklahoma City to judge the state fair's Shorthorn show, was among the victims of an armed robbery. Listed as stolen was a diamond ring valued at $2,000, other items of jewelry worth another $1900, and several hundred in cash.

The following article appeared in the Telegraph in early December, 1921:

*Three men who took part in a holdup in Oklahoma City last*
*fall where Harry Hopley lost a $2,000 diamond ring are again at*

*large as the result of a ruse pulled by a friend of theirs in which
he doped the chief of police at Oklahoma City with a narcotic
cigarette and escaped with the evidence and the prisoners.*

*The men were arrested in connection with the robbery of
a mail car on the Santa Fe Railroad near Edmond, Oklahoma
and fingerprints were found on the bottles which contained the
explosives they used.*

*One of the men in Oklahoma City who was robbed at the
same time Hopley was, identified these men as the ones who
entered the house where the robbery occurred and ordered the
victims to "stick 'em up."*

The jail break story is suspect. The chief of police would not have
been personally attending prisoners, and the "narcotic cigarette" was
probably a fabrication. More likely, a cohort of the suspects bribed
a jailer, who used being "doped" as an excuse for his inattentiveness.
The gang, apprehended after robbing a mail car with the use of high
explosives, was not the sort to pull a random mugging. There's more to
this story than was printed, and we learn a part of it later.

We don't know if Harry's diamond ring was insured, but his brother's
house was. On a cold night in mid-January of 1922 a fire broke out
in the basement of the nearly new brick frame structure. The blaze
was apparently caused by a malfunction in what was called the house's
"complete electric plant." (Calling the system a "complete electrical
plant" was not an overstatement. Rural electricity, supplied by a power
plant in Atlantic, would not be available for several years. Wayland had
a generator. Harry, when he built a few years earlier for Della, went
with gas lighting. Times were changing.)

Helen and Wayland were alerted early. Neither they nor baby George
were endangered by a fire that spread slowly at first. One of them rang
up central and the Lewis Volunteer Fire Department responded with
what was called a "chemical truck."

The Lewis department had a modern, gasoline powered fire truck.
An issue at the time was that these trucks, though marginally better for
the purpose than horse-drawn apparatus, were small. Water is heavy.

The shifting weight of liquid makes it more difficult to transport than solids. Accessing an adequate supply of water in rural areas far from city water hydrants was, if the fire was of any size, all but impossible. In an attempt to overcome these problems, chemicals were used. Some were added to water in the truck's water tank. Others, such as acid and baking soda, were introduced into a sealed container in which a chemical reaction created a pressurized extinguisher. So-called "chemical fire trucks" of the time were equipped with one or more devices intended to make the limited amount of water more effective.

As fire ate its way up the basement stairs and through the wood floor, the Lewis department was soon out of water, their extinguishers empty. Before this happened, a call went to the Atlantic Department. Such a call today would result in trucks and men on the road within minutes. This request, however, was denied. Atlantic's city council had in the past seen their department leave town and didn't like it. The whole concept of who would pay for expensive firefighting equipment, and who would be protected by it, was under debate in the 19-teens and twenties—and even today.

Atlantic's mayor, a man named Coomes, along with a councilman named Jones, had a hasty conference. In their view, sending firemen and equipment to the Hopley place left the city in peril should a fire take place in town.

Whether Atlantic's department could have done much good under the best of circumstances is of doubt. They'd have gotten there well after Lewis, and they had the same water shortage problems. The time taken to debate whether to send them rendered them even less likely to be of value.

There was an irony noted by some—and almost certainly the family. Only months after an Atlantic newspaper, as had been done a dozen times before, lauded the Hopley family for *"putting Cass County on the map,"* the county seat town denied a plea for help. Charles Willey, who felt Lewis had been dealt to from the bottom of the deck when the seat of county government was taken away, when roads bypassed her, had another illustration.

The house, valued at $10,000, not including contents that added a few thousand more, was fully insured. Most of the exterior walls and foundation were intact, the interior was rebuilt, and Helen essentially had a second new house just three years after moving into the first.

In the spring of 1922 a corporation called The Atlantic Shipping Association leased the grain elevator at the Hopley Switch, and Thomas Hopley saw his name in the paper in a manner he would not have preferred. He'd purchased a farm in Taylor County in 1920. There was a lien in the amount of $7,500 held by a man named Frank Rathje. Rathje's lawsuit alleged that Hopley, as part of the contract purchase, agreed to pay the lien. He was, according to Rathje, nearly two years overdue.

A few days after being served, Thomas Hopley filed a petition of his own. This one called for a foreclosure on an Atlantic man named Simunic and his wife, who had bought property from Hopley on a contract and had fallen behind in payments. The judgment asked for was $4,500.

Things were not going well for Thomas, who was soon to begin experiencing the heart problems that ended his life. Peter, then seventy-five, was himself quite ill during much of March. Suffering from pneumonia, he was sick enough long enough that friends and family feared he might not recover.

Another indicator that times were changing appeared above the fold in an edition that included an update on Peter's health.

*District Engineer L.M. Martin has the distinction of receiving the first aerial music over his radiophone at his home last night.*

*Last week Mr. Martin constructed his aerial. He was then quite busy for a few days. Last night, with the assistance of Harold Hawthorne, who was in the Naval Wireless Service during the late war, they completed installation of the equipment.*

*At about 8 o'clock the tune-up process began. Several interferences were encountered until they reached the 370 meter wave length. There they caught the announcement of a musical program to be broadcast by an Omaha station, the identity of which could not be distinguished. Following the announcement the saxophone music began. The first piece was Wabash Blues.*

*The Des Moines Register was also to broadcast a musical program that evening, but their station could not be heard.*

The article, which doesn't make it clear whether the music was the first heard on a radio in Atlantic, or just the first heard on Martin's, concluded by saying that with additional tuning and adjustment of equipment, the "radiophone" would be able to pick up broadcasts from even greater distances.

Harry received good news in April: the armed bandits had been recaptured and would stand trial. He boarded a train for Oklahoma City to testify. We learn, from the Daily Oklahoman, that E.F. Harriff and his wife were entertaining Hopley and W.W. Furse of Ft. Worth (he also being a Shorthorn judge). He and Hopley were in town to preside over the national Shorthorn show. Harry Hopley, Furse, and Mr. and Mrs. Harriff were in the parlor when, at about 11:15 pm, two men (the Telegraph apparently erred in saying there were three) wielding guns entered the house. The four victims were lined up facing a wall. While one bandit held a gun on them, the other stripped them of valuables. This article lists Hopley's ring as being worth $3,500. Hopley also had a bit more than $500 cash taken from him. The robbers fled. Someone in the house had a revolver. Furse grabbed it, raced to the door and fired a shot or two at the fleeing pair, but must have missed.

Harry's younger brother would, forty years later, have an eerily similar experience.

Peter remained sick most of the summer. Pneumonia gave way to grippe and concern that he might not survive lingered. He was bedfast in his home on Oregon Street, under a nurse's care. It seems safe to assume the local papers had his obituary ready to print.

Peter's illness was only part of a bad season. Margaret's husband, a young man still in his forties, took a nasty fall in their home. Lumsden broke both arms and badly twisted a knee. Having a husband with two broken arms was painful for him, presumably unpleasant for Margaret. Knowing Judge Kenesaw Mountain Landis, in this instance, did them no good.

Della, in what may offer a hint as to why she and Harry had no children, rode with her husband to Rochester, Minnesota. There she underwent *"the surgical removal of a tumor."*

Things took a turn for the better in the fall. Harry was appointed supervisor of swine at the county fair. Della was home from Rochester. Peter was improved—he was not yet up to leaving the house, but he was out of bed and had found his appetite.

# Chapter Seventeen

Peter was back in good health in 1924, but Della, his daughter-in-law, was not feeling the best. He went to California in the spring, as had become his custom, to *"look into his California property."* She went to Excelsior Springs, taking Eleanor with her. Della and the girl stayed at "The Royal," touted as being the most exclusive spa in the area. Harry stayed home to look after business, have another Shorthorn "special sale," this one at the Rock Island Depot sale pavilion. Peter returned, sold a couple of building lots in Atlantic, acting as bondsman when the Bank of Lewis closed. (This closing was headline news in several papers. The Cass County bank of Lewis had gone under in the 1890s, resulting in the Dickerson trial. It was re-opened under Hopley's friend and neighbor, W.J. Harris, and was viewed as a solid institution for several years. After Harris retired the bank, one of two then operating in Lewis, had W.W. Albright as president, Frank Albright, cashier, and Wilbert Albert was assistant cashier. The reason for closing, which occurred after a meeting which reportedly lasted late into the night, was "frozen paper." The bank was closed only about a month, being reorganized as the Citizen's State Bank of Lewis, with W.J. Woodward the president.)

The big event in the Hopley family that year took place in May.

Wayland Arrowsmith Hopley, Jr., came into the world on May 24, 1924. Wayland and Helen named their first-born George, reserving the "Junior" designation for their second child.

Thirty-four years later Wayland, Sr., sat at a desk in the office of "Hopco," a truck stop his second son had to have, and tearfully told a bewildered, seventeen-year-old part-time bookkeeper named Emily Blakely, *"I wish I'd taken that boy the day he was born, put him in a sack, dropped him off the river bridge and let him drown."* George's younger brothers disappointed a lot of people.

Peter, the old, hard-working pioneer, was not universally liked. We assume jealousy was a factor for some, others disapproved of his life-style. He was, some felt, not as charitable as he might have been, and otheers found him less than pleasant to work for. Most of the negative things said about him and Edna did not make the papers—offending Peter Hopley was not in an editor's best interest.

One nettling negative was a persistent allegation that he'd gotten where he was more through luck than labor. Peter Hopley wrote at various times this was being said of him. He defended himself by frequent mentions of how hard he'd worked, which didn't convince those who preferred to think otherwise. At times when Peter was interviewed, which was often, he was quick to tell of how he'd worked harder than pretty much anyone he knew. Espousing this in the 1880s and 90s, with the days he was referring to in the recent past, was one thing. Doing so in the 19-teens and twenties, with his hair thinning and his waist expanding, was another. When he went out in November of 1918 and picked corn, snapping the ears from stalks, shucking them, tossing them against the "bangboard," he did so for recreation, for the nostalgia. The fact that his few minutes of physical work made the news indicates this was a rare event. Peter Hopley, in reality, had probably not experienced a labor-induced sweat for decades. There was no point in doing so—such had long-since ceased to be his role. It was easy for those who didn't approve of him anyway to say they'd never seen the man work a day in his life. They hadn't.

Charles Hunt, long-time managing editor of the News Telegraph, found a way to defend Hopley without going out of his way to do so. Hunt was, in the mid-1920s, doing a series of articles on long-time subscribers. In July of 1924 he chose as his subject two authentic pioneers of Cass County; Mr. and Mrs. T.R. Worth. Of them he wrote:

*"I had a most pleasant visit yesterday with Mr. and Mrs. T.R. Worth of Lewis, two of the worthiest of that town's many worthy people. These good people came to the county back in 1854, Mr. Worth coming here in an ox team from Ohio and Mrs. Worth coming from a nearby county when but four years old. They have both lived in the vicinity ever since and the years have looked kindly upon them.*

*Talking of the primitive days of this section, Mr. and Mrs. Worth said that school houses were miles apart and roads, as we know them, or any approach thereto, entirely unknown. Nearest neighbors were miles away.*

*Friendships were strong and life was full of romance, even with the work of subduing the wilderness as the county was then.*

*Mr. Worth said he had hunted horses all over where Atlantic is now located long before Atlantic was thought of. He worked as a boy for the late Isaac Dickerson and was a boyhood friend of Peter Hopley and the "Hopley boys."*

*He said the story going around that Peter has never done any hard work was a piece of fiction, as he had worked with him and knew.*

*These people have been friends of the Telegraph family ever since Lafe Young founded the Telegraph. . . . "* and so on.

The article concluded with flowery language regarding the *"galaxy of subscribers"* who had laid the foundations for life as it was through their hard work.

Life as it was then was good. The "Roaring Twenties" were not to Cass County what they were to New York and Chicago, but good times rolled. The business of business was making money and there was money to be made. Investors in bonds were doing well—those in stocks amassing great wealth—and doing so without working at all. Grain and cattle prices were not what farmers wanted—they never were. Harry spoke of the need to conserve, to cut back where possible, to feed only thrifty animals (he probably had his "grass-fed" Hampshires in mind), and to make conservative investments. Wayland, it appears, did not entirely share those views.

1924 and '25 were comparatively uneventful, although the Hopleys were ensnarled in a number of lawsuits. Wayland was sued by a motorist who struck a Hopley steer that had wandered onto the White Pole Road near the farm. How the steer got out was unknown, but we can be confident the reason wasn't because of an inadequate fence post. As a result of another accident, Harry was sued by C.T. Davis, the owner and driver of a Ford that had been demolished in a collision with Hopley's Overland Roadster a few months before. Harry countersued, claiming the mishap was the fault of Davis. (Harry Hopley may have been a bit like Harry Rae when it came to switching from buggies to automobiles. Hopley didn't go into the depression Rae did, but was involved in more than his share of collisions.)

Both brothers were called to Omaha to testify in a lawsuit filed against Rock Island by a motorist whose car was mangled by a southbound train near the Hopley Switch. The Hopleys were called only because they'd witnessed the accident.

Harry won his lawsuit. Wayland lost, but the jury was sympathetic, rendering a judgment of only $40 and costs.

In a news item so typical the typesetter need only change the date, Colonel N.G. Kraschel of Atlantic, the noted auctioneer, cried the sale of several hundred head of Colorado feeder calves. Oscar Otto, an employee (and later president) of the Whitney Bank, was clerk. Harry Hopley managed the crew working corrals and loading out. The biggest buyers were Peter and Wayland Hopley, who picked up sixty-four head at a total cost of $5,789.

The sale, held in early September, would be repeated a month later. More western calves, more of Colonel Kraschel, more of the Hopleys taking home several choice lots of calves.

A noteworthy ad, next to the sale results, was a listing of radio programs. When District Engineer Martin set up his aerial and "radiophone" a couple of years earlier and, in a story worthy of the front page, tuned in "Wabash Blues," radio was a rarity. Now so many readers had the devices that a program schedule sold newspapers.

Peter went to California for the winter, where he continued to *"hold substantial land interests."* He left his vineyards and irrigated fields in the northern part of the state in January, going south to San Diego to spend time with friends and wait for spring.

Helen and Della were, by then, into bridge. They joined a club, meeting at the home of the hostess of the week, having a fine lunch, drawing for partners, then settling in for an afternoon of cards. Helen also enjoyed canasta, and insisted Wayland learn to play.

Harry, in the spring of 1925, took his wife to the Lewis Alumni Banquet. While he'd graduated from Lewis High School with the class of 1899, his affiliations were more closely based in Atlantic. Peter commuted from Lewis to the farm. Harry, living on the farm, playing football with the Maroons, buying and selling livestock at sales held either at the Rock Island Depot sale pavilion or a similar facility at the fairgrounds, was naturally drawn more to Atlantic than Lewis. He had his classmates, though, and friends, and was a regular at the annual gathering of alumni.

In March of 1926 Harry Hopley, upon learning of his father's illness, boarded a train for California. He arrived too late, could only accompany the body on the train ride back to Iowa.

Harry, it seems, took a lot of trips that didn't work out as planned, one of which—a year after his father's death—was reported by the press His brother was a companion.

*An experience not down on the sale bills and one they do not care to repeat was that of Harry and Wayland Hopley, well-known stock raisers of this county, on the occasion of a trip last week to South Dakota to buy feeder cattle.*

*They pounded gumbo, forded a swollen river, got off the trail and were lost and had about all the untoward things happen to them they care to for some little time.*

*They lost the trail when they turned the wrong way north of Belle Fourche, South Dakota, and after wandering for about 100 miles forded a swollen river in which they almost got their car stuck. After Harry plunged in to test the depth of the stream they went on and found themselves, tired and muddy and disgusted, near the town of Albion, Montana.*

*They found their way from there back to a road which led to Rapid City, South Dakota, and reached there in time to be present when President Coolidge addressed a big gathering of*

*Indians.  On Sunday they went to church in Rapid City where the President did.  From Rapid City they did their scouting for feeder cattle.  They returned yesterday after buying 1,000 head.*

*The Hopleys are glad to be home again and say while Iowa roads can stand surfacing they have those in South Dakota beaten to death.  They made nearly the entire trip on the way there in the rain.  They traveled a total of 2,500 miles.  On the return trip they made an average of 30 miles per hour, but on the way up in the rain, they made but 80 miles in the whole day. (Atlantic News Telegraph, August 17, 1927)*

Wayland was experienced and established by the time his father died.  He was a young man, a WW 1 veteran, and he thought big.  It was probably not a coincidence that the Hopley Elevator was founded a couple of years after Wayland became a partner.

1926, though, was not a time for grand ideas.  There were more immediate problems.  Peter's estate was somewhat of a snarl. He had taken steps to reduce the tax liability on his heirs—to see that as much of his estate as possible went to the family and not the government.  This seems to have entailed verbal agreements; sales that were on paper only.  His will had the standard equal share provisions.  This was complicated, however, by what he'd given some of his offspring before his passing.  There was the mansion, a gift to Margaret, as was the California property.  He intended for an equal value to go to other heirs.  This included farmland and livestock he'd bought on shares with the sons.  Family members wanted no more than equity; the problem was in coming to terms as to just what that was.

The situation was complicated by lawsuits.  Edith was then fifty, married to Clarence Hedges, and living in south-central Iowa.  A suit was filed by a Des Moines resident asking that the transfer of real estate from the late Peter Hopley to Harry and Wayland be set aside because he, the plaintiff, held a lien against Hedges.  Assuming she was in line for an inheritance, the plaintiff wanted his money before disbursement of the estate proceeded.  In April the Anita bank got into the act.  They also held a note against the Hedges.  The ink on this is blurry—the amount appears to have been either $3,000 or $8,000—and the bank filed to assign judgment to Wayland. Wayland, in the transfer of certain real estate from Peter to him (presumably farm property) agreed to pay, within ten years, both Margaret and Edith the sum of $25,000.

Each brother had their own independent operation. They also had ongoing dealings in partnership with Peter, as well as some in shares with each other. Other suits were filed. Those to whom family members owed a debt, or were alleged to, took steps to assure payment as a part of estate settlement. Everything would work out—it just took time and lawyers.

In the spring of 1927, Harry Hopley presided over a meeting that furthered a cause he had long had an interest in; the snake-like East Nishnabotna. The Hopleys had land on both sides of the river and were among those who dealt with high water more years than not. The river looped and curved and doubled back, and within each loop were little twists. The East Nishnabotna, it was said, traveled ten miles in what a straight line would cover in two. Floods were a common occurrence. A good many people wanted the beast tamed. Straightening it, they believed, was the way. Eliminate the bends that slowed flow, move water down a relatively straight channel, and the problem would be solved. A group of farmers formed an informal organization to work toward this end. At a meeting held in March, Harry Hopley presiding as chairman, progress was made. County supervisors Malone and Zellmer were there. Harry Hopley was supported by other "heavy landowners," including F.R. Hunt, Wayland Hopley, and J.W. Cuykendall.

With backing like this, the Telegraph reported, *"This will be the last year that floods will hamper travel on roads to Atlantic."*

A few days later Harry had the distinction of topping the Omaha cattle market with a load of choice steers. Bob Roush had done his work well. The steers had been on full feed for six months—feed that included not just corn, but protein supplements. Cattle not yet two years old had averaged 1,077 pounds and brought $11.60 per hundred. A month later he shipped five more rail car loads. Wayland was not far behind, sending four. The following week Wayland had another shipment.

Della, then having lived in their home for twenty years, felt it was time for new furniture. Topping the Omaha market signaled an opportunity to pose the question to Harry. Furniture to their taste—or at least Della's—apparently could not be found in Atlantic. They asked Arthur Young, described as Atlantic's foremost "furniture leader," to accompany them to Rock Island, Illinois. They returned with the best to be found.

While Harry and Della were selecting furniture, Wayland and Helen took a vacation of several weeks in Minnesota. They were accompanied by Howard Marshall. Marshall was arguably one of the best athletes ever to graduate from Atlantic high school, and became a leading businessman. He starred in multiple sports, led his college football team, and was good enough in baseball to be signed to a professional contract. He met his match, though, and couldn't hit a major league curve ball. Back in Atlantic he worked for a time in the auto dealership owned by Clyde Herring. (Herring, who would later become governor, was well-acquainted with the Hopley family, especially Peter and Edna. His wife and Edna had been, if not close friends, at least regulars on the reception, tea, and card party circuit.)

In about 1920 Marshall teamed up with W.E. Kelloway of Anita, who founded the Walnut Grove Feed Company. Marshall's title was manager until 1925, when he was named vice-president. In 1927, the year he and Wayland Hopley vacationed in Minnesota, Walnut Grove moved to Atlantic. We seem safe to assume Marshall and Hopley talked about livestock and feed. Hopley and his brother were the county's leading producers of hogs and cattle. All understood the importance of rapid gains, of feed supplements that achieved this while lowering, or at least not increasing, the cost. The fact that Walnut Grove Research Farms was built near Wayland's home, on land purchased from him, was probably in the planning stages during their joint vacation.

Wayland was back from his business vacation with Howard Marshall in time to take his wife to Iowa City for college homecoming festivities.

The drainage project moved, but not very fast and not entirely the way some would have liked. Wayland was chair of the horse-pulling contest in Atlantic in the summer of 1928. He was also seeing a lawyer. His suit alleged that the drainage contractor tore out fences and trees that were not necessary to the project, and failed to provide compensation.

Had he been able to foresee the future, the manner in which he met his death, he likely would have asked that plank bridges over drainage ditches be built in a manner that afforded more safety.

Harry and Wayland got along well, had the mutual trust and respect to jointly purchase 500 acres at a price that, although not disclosed, was probably double what their father's ceiling on Iowa land value had been.

In Cass County, the purchase was the big farm news story of 1928. Hopley farms, already the main player in the local livestock business, had just gotten bigger. The J.W. Berry estate was south of Marne, good land with a fine house and outbuildings. Buying in the location they did was a departure—all other Harry and Wayland Hopley farmland (excluding that in other states) was adjoining.

Newspapers took the sale as an opportunity to expound, once again, on the magnitude of the Hopley operation. Their land in Cass County totaled, at that point, about 2,800 acres. According to the Telegraph, there was not another farming partnership or joint operation in the county as large. Ten married men with families worked for Hopley full time. Dozens of day laborers were hired during the summer. In 1927 they'd shipped 157 carloads of fat cattle out of Hopley Station, most of them bound for markets in Chicago. (This presents a question: how many fat cattle to a rail car? It depends, of course, on their size and that of the car. When Peter began shipping cattle rail cars typically held 20,000 pounds of beef on the hoof. Cars got bigger. By the early 1900s cars that would haul 60,000 pounds were common. The type of cattle Hopleys fed were generally fat at about 1,000 pounds. 157 carloads is a lot of beef.)

They had nearly 200 head of purebred cows from which they sold breeding and show stock, plus a couple of hundred head of cross-bred stock cows. At any one time they might have between 1,500 and 2,000 hogs. Their elevator at Hopley Station had a 40,000 bushel capacity. They raised hundreds of acres of corn (900 acres were in corn the year before), but fed so much stock they bought corn a thousand bushel at a time. They were using a couple of tractors, but still farmed extensively with horses. The term "picture place" was used by reporters, as was "Hopley Ranch." (This was an informal title. Harry had his place,

Wayland his, and they owned land and other investments jointly. Reporters tended to lump it together and refer to the entirety as "Hopley Ranch.")

Harry's cement posts were picturesque, as were the neatly painted and tended outbuildings. The houses were Hopley houses, the barns likewise, and nothing more need be said.

That year, with the purchase of the 500 acre Berry estate, marked a high for the Hopley operation in terms of Iowa acres owned. The future looked bright. There was, however, a Great Depression ahead, and a war that would take the heirs apparent.

# Chapter Eighteen

Buying 500 acres of farm land is a risk. Buying that land several miles from the home place, at a time when farming was still primarily reliant on horses, made the venture more challenging. Buying at a time when land prices had, in the seventy years since their grandfather bought at $25 an acre, risen almost continuously year after year was pressing one's luck.

Another issue was Peter's way of doing business, which was not unlike that of most others in similar occupation. He made much of his money while borrowing it. Edna had her health cycles; Peter's were in borrowing. Once he was established, no local bank would turn him down. His system worked, by and large, as it was supposed to. He'd borrow a few thousand, buy a load of calves, borrow more for feed. When the fat cattle sold he'd repay the loan. The profit went into wages, buildings, fences, more land, and the cycle started again. While he was a man worth a million and more, he went to a banker in order to spend a thousand. His sons did business the same way. The Depression, though, changed that. Money, once easy to borrow for the Hopley brothers, became tight. Loans were being called. The brothers would, before the Depression ended, find it necessary to sell land to acquire operating principal.

The year after Harry and Wayland bought the Berry place was one that started like most others. In February Harry was in Chicago judging a Shorthorn show. It was announced that numerous rural homes and outbuildings, including those of Wayland and Thomas, would soon be wired for electricity from the new Atlantic plant.

Harry returned from Chicago, but was not long at home. The Ak-Sar-Ben stock show would soon be underway, and once again he was in charge of the cattle department.

Wayland, who during those years was more or less constantly snarled in one lawsuit or another, was defending one filed by a certain J.P. Plunkett. Plunkett, a salesman for the Service Life Insurance Company of Lincoln, had sold Wayland a $5,000 life insurance policy. Wayland signed a note for the premium, payable in March of 1927. Hopley apparently had second thoughts. He didn't pay. Hopley acknowledged the note, but his lawyer pointed out in court that "the note did not specify on its face that it was given as an insurance premium."

What? Hopley signed the application for a life insurance policy, agreed to a note providing for payment. He then told the court he refused to pay because "the note did not specify that it was given as an insurance premium." This, on the surface, seems to have been the thinnest of technicalities. Hopley had made an obligation. The premium was a drop in the Hopley bucket.

This was a time, though, when insurance salesmen went door-to-door. Some were fast-talking sharpies. Plunkett may have been one of them. It is also true that a few insurance companies of that time commonly made farm loans. They had capital, wanted to get a solid return, and farmers with collateral were a preferred risk. To get the best of both worlds, insurance companies could require a loan applicant to insure the loan with a life insurance policy—from their company.

When the Hopleys borrowed from a life insurance company, it was usually Metro Life of Kansas City. One would have expected that, had Wayland wished to take out a policy on his life, he'd have chosen them.

Whatever the details, the Cass County District Court found in Hopley's favor. Service Life Insurance Company, no doubt more concerned about the precedent than the comparatively trivial amount of premium, appealed to Iowa's Supreme Court. The Supreme Court heard the case and ruled the state's insurance law had been misconstrued by district court, reversing the decision in favor of Plunkett. Wayland Hopley had to pay, plus court costs.

If he was upset, he took it out on local sportsmen. A paid ad in the Telegraph in September of 1929 stated the Hopley brothers had posted their land. Their 3,000 acres had been open to hunters—at least those who asked. No more. The ad claimed that hunters had *"taken advantage of our good nature, and been careless to the point of posing a threat to livestock and buildings."* Hopley land was off-limits; there'd be no more hunting and violators would be prosecuted.

The Telegraph felt the measure, given the amount of acreage involved, rated a front page story. They ran it on October 4, next to one announcing the suicide of *"Fred Porterfield, well-known proprietor of the Budweiser Soft Drink and Billiards Parlor in Atlantic."* Porterfield, who lived alone in an apartment above his pool hall, was found there with his head in the oven and the gas turned on.

When prohibition was enacted in 1920 his Budweiser Saloon became a Budweiser soft drink establishment. The Budweiser name did not lend itself well to the sale of soda pop. Porterfield's saloon became a billiard parlor and cigar store. The article does not give the reason for Porterfield's decision to shorten his life, but implies business was not good. If this was a factor, Porterfield should have held out for a while—Prohibition was soon to be repealed.

On the same day, below the fold, was a small item saying the stock market in New York *"was in turmoil."*

The market crash did not have an immediate effect on rural southwest Iowa. Economic downturns were cyclical and this one was assumed to be another bump in the road. The 1930 model Nash went on sale just days after the crash, with Cass County buyers willing to pay $915 for the lower-priced version; over $1,600 for the deluxe model.

In November Wayland expanded on his decision to shift to Black Angus cattle. Harry was Shorthorns and Herefords, along with a few Angus-cross cows. Wayland preferred straight Angus, and took two rail cars of them to the Chicago stock show. They did well and were, from that point on, the breed of choice for Wayland Hopley and his sons.

One of those sons, Wayland Jr., celebrated his sixth birthday with a party at the Hopley home. Several classmates were invited and, according to a news item, found *"Young Wayland Jr. to be the best host in Iowa and they wish him many happy returns."* Hickory Hopley may not have actually been the best host in Iowa, but he did like to party.

So did his father. He and an Atlantic appliance dealer named Harold Schrauger teamed up to throw a holiday-season "stag party" at the farm. Eighteen men attended, dined on duck and pheasant, circumvented prohibition, and a *"rousing good time was had by all."*

Circumventing prohibition was not that difficult. In September of 1930, an Omaha man was pulled over near Atlantic for driving too fast. In his car was found 85 gallons of alcohol. He was one of the few who were caught.

Later that month the bank in Grant failed to open. Depositors, learning too late, could only hope.

The Atlantic Rotary Club was temporarily more interested in weeds than either booze or the stock market. Carl Goeken, Atlantic H.S. agriculture teacher (who also owned a large parcel of farmland adjoining Riverside Farm and was the father of "Froggy" Goeken), challenged his class with a weed contest. Students were sent on field trips, including one to Hopley farms, then were graded on such things as identifying various species, display, mounting, neatness, and a written essay on eradication. Awards were given during a Rotary meeting, after which club member W. Carney Martin gave a presentation on the Wayland Hopley farming operation. Wayland Hopley, he said, was himself farming 1,200 acres, feeding 1,000 fat cattle each year (all of Angus breeding),and was then preparing for both the Ak-Sar-Ben stock show in Omaha and the national competition in Chicago. He had six full-time employees, numerous seasonal ones, and bought any surplus corn in the vicinity for *"above market price."*

Not everyone, as we shall see, agreed with that statement.

Club president Harry Hopley, who had a somewhat larger operation than his younger brother, did not say so. He led in singing the closing song, then called for adjournment.

Harry spent much of January, 1931, in Montana and Idaho, where he had "business interests." There is no record of the family owning land there, so he was probably contracting for feeder calves. He'd seen temperatures, he told reporters after returning, dip to forty below.

In March the Colonel presided over another Hopley auction. With Kraschel (who was soon to become Iowa's Lt. Governor) at the gavel, with 6,000 people reportedly in attendance, Harry Hopley sold bred gilts, yearling Shorthorn bulls (mostly of Village Beau or Browndale Goldspur bloodlines), machinery, seed oats, and the big attraction—66 head of Belgian horses, many of them registered. The number included a few mules, well trained, hard workers with Belgian breeding.

Overall, the sale went well. Bulls brought a good price, a couple of stallions over $500 each. The only unfortunate incident took place as a yearling colt was being led into the sale ring. Something startled the horse. It bolted, broke away from its handler, and charged through a throng of bystanders. Several were knocked to the ground and injured, none seriously. Harry, his home equipped with electricity and a telephone line, may have used the latter go give his lawyer a heads up.

The sale bill lists the location of the sale as being "6 miles southwest of Atlantic to the Hopley grain elevator, then 1 mile west." Later sales were held in Carl Goeken's barn, which he didn't use. The Hopleys renovated the barn, putting in an auctioneer's station, sale ring, and bleachers.

The year was perhaps the Hopley brothers' best to date in terms of stock show winnings. Harry swept the important ribbons with Shorthorns at the Illinois state fair. Wayland showed Angus and won. Both exhibited and won again in September. In the Ak-Sar-Ben show in November Harry had the top Shorthorn bull, Wayland the best Angus. They rounded out the year with another winning performance at the National show in Chicago.

1931 was also the year Thomas died. Jennie, then sixty-six, had moved back to the farm and helped care for him. When his condition worsened she had him taken to the home of her sister and brother-in-law.

Thomas passed peacefully on the 4th of March in the home of Sophia and Dr. Campbell. There came another assessment, another will, another estate to settle.

During that settlement an indication of Jennie Hopley's wealth was disclosed. She was frugal for a lifetime, and did quite well. At various times she was a housekeeper, a nurse, an accountant. She had an eighth grade education, was never in a position to make more than a living wage. William had left her some rental property in Atlantic and she received a share of Thomas's profits (when he had them). She retained that and made safe investments. Thomas sold some of their father's land. She received a share, saved some and re-invested. She bought land, probably part of what Frank farmed, in South Dakota. When Thomas died Frank was named manager of the Cass County farm, but a ¼ share of it was hers. Jennie wasn't a socialite, rarely made the news, traveled little. Never married, childless, serving as mother to her siblings when Mary died, spending much of her life with Thomas, also unmarried, she was attached to Frank's children and grandchildren. As Frank's older daughters married while in South Dakota and remained there, she saw little of them. Tommy, though, then a tow-headed eleven-year-old, moved to the home place with his parents. Jennie welcomed Frank back, and her attachment to Tommy grew. She was there, his dear Aunt Jennie, to see him off at the depot when he went to war.

Sophia died in Atlantic in 1943. Jennie, 79, passed on a year later. She left a sizeable estate, could have lived in a more opulent manner than she did. Her will was standard for an unmarried person; equal shares to her brother, her sisters preceding her in death had their shares divided between their children.

Tommy, when Jennie died, was in the South Pacific. As preparations were being made for her funeral he saw his first kamikaze attack.

On the 7th of October, 1931, the day Thomas Hopley was buried, Helen Hopley gave birth to her and Wayland's third son. Peter William checked into the world, the paper tells us, weighing an even nine pounds.

There was something about Helen's babies that seemed to attract fire. Nearly ten years before George had been an infant when the house was gutted by a fire that originated in the basement. Peter William was but six months old when fire again did damage. This time the blaze, which started in the kitchen as the result of either a malfunction or misuse of the kerosene range, caused only minor damage.

Fire districting and procedure had changed. Atlantic's department, as directed by the mayor and council, had refused to respond to the first house fire. This decision was subject to criticism. The Hopleys had done a great deal for Atlantic. Volunteer firemen do not join a department in order to stay in town while the home of one of the area's most prominent citizens goes up in smoke.

Some of the same men were on the department when the second call came. They rolled out with lights and siren blaring, as did members of the Lewis department. Neither, it turns out, were needed. Wayland and Helen smothered the blaze with blankets. By the time firefighters arrived there was no fire to fight. Helen showed off baby Peter, and firefighters returned home.

Harry and Wayland had a mortgage on 500 acres and were feeding cattle on borrowed money. The Depression settled in and land was, within a few years, worth a fraction of what they'd paid. Fat cattle brought less than their price as calves, grain crops nearly worthless. Banks, those that stayed open, all but stopped loaning money.

The Hopley brothers were, along with most everyone else, in a tight spot. If things were worse for them it was due to heavy debt and the size of their operation. Harry spoke publicly of cutting back, reducing expenses. Wayland was slower to change.

The Iowa-born Republican, Herbert Hoover, failed in his re-election bid because Democrats promised to make things better—a New Deal. The size of government, and government programs, ballooned. Republicans could say the country had been through bad times before and recovered, that FDR and his deficit spending were making things worse. Democrats responded that Republican policies got the county into a mess that would have been much worse had not they, the Democrats, taken measures.

Economic conditions did not put a stop to social affairs. Atlantic had an active P.E.O. (Philanthropic Educational Organization) club. This women's organization was, and is, an advocate of better opportunities and education for woman. Helen Hopley was a long-time member. In January of 1932 the regular meeting was held at the home of Mrs. Oscar Otto (he being the long-time president of the Whitney bank), where Helen Hopley gave a program on 'Founder's Day.' The program was probably a good one. The founding of P.E.O. dates to the late 1860s—the time of Susan B. Anthony, Elizabeth Cady Stanton, and others involved in the suffrage movement. For some reason it was decided that the meaning of "P.E.O." would forever be a secret. Only members, who underwent and participated in secret rituals could know. Helen Haw Hopley knew her history, was proud of her family ties to the Revolutionary War, and no doubt gave a fine program.

In February the big event at Hopley's Switch was a train derailment. An early thaw and some horse-drawn wagons crossing the tracks on a dirt road just south of the switch had left a good deal of mud on the rails. The mud stiffened overnight and at 8 a.m., when the southbound train hit it, the result was bad. Six cars, including one passenger, one coal, the others freight, derailed. None, however, overturned. Mail for Lewis and Griswold was picked up at the scene and taken by automobile to the respective post offices (ATN, Feb. 19, 1932).

A month later Wayland took thirty-some head of his 1931 show stock to the Atlantic Fairgrounds for a much-advertised sale, again with Col. N.G. Kraschel auctioneering.

At about the same time Governor Dan Turner made a trip to Atlantic, where he was speaker at a Rotary Club meeting held at the Calumet café. Turner spoke of bad times and depressed prices, and stated a case in favor of the government supporting corn to 60c a bushel (corn, that year, went as low as 20c a bushel). He said when he'd gone to Washington to state his case he'd met with objections at the federal level. Turner cited a meeting with a member of the Federal Reserve Board who argued that Iowa farmers should be happy with 20 to 30 cent corn as it made for inexpensive hog and cattle feed. Here Turner referred to the Hopley brothers. The Hopleys, he said, raise thousands of bushels of corn, but "they buy five or six times as much as the ordinary raiser. And yet they are in favor of fair prices for corn as they understand that livestock prices always follow that of corn." (ATN, Feb. 16, 1932)

The Depression was deepening and farmers, including the Hopley brothers, were hurting. Both, particularly Wayland, continued to spend heavily on expensive bulls and livestock shows. Harry tried a resumption of the horse importation business.

Peter had loved his Suffolk Punches. With Harry it was Belgians. He'd predicted when the war broke out that it would take two decades for the horse trade to recover. Thirty years passed until, in 1937, he bought nearly 30 draft animals of the Belgiun breed, bringing them back on a ship of the Red Star Line. A news article on the purchase says the horses were taken to Hoboken, New Jersey, where they were met by *"Cab Marker of Lewis, an employee of the Hopley place,"* for return to the farm. Marker was, at that time, in partnership with his father in a hardware store in Lewis. He was probably not a Hopley employee, other than doing their plumbing and heating. He took this trip to pick up a few dollars and, at the same time, to stop in Chicago and visit a brother who was then living there. Most of the horses were sold at auction a few weeks later.

Whether Harry made money on this deal was not disclosed, but that he kept, imported, and sold fine representatives of the breed probably helped make them locally popular. My grandfather had a team of Belgians. I delivered papers to a man named Purdue who kept a long-retired team of Belgians on his acreage in north-central Lewis. The Bode brothers west of town were farming into the 1950s with a team that had Belgian coloring. Harry Wheatley plowed garden plots in Lewis with a pair of cross-bred Belgians. Peter's Suffolk Punch were not so popular.

While we don't know what Harry paid for his imported horses, or what he sold them for, there probably wasn't a lot of profit. Not many farmers had the money to buy blooded, high-dollar stallions. But tough as the Depression years were, the Hopley operation gave the appearance of prosperity. Bob Kennedy is of the opinion that Harry and Wayland held things together, in part, by methods that were not entirely ethical— or even legal.

He remembers Harry Hopley doing much of his cursing from the back of a horse. Others preferred a buggy, but not Harry. He had his cattle and his Belgian horses and, Kennedy said, his brushes with creditors. "He came over one day and asked dad (Lou Kennedy) to do him a favor." A banker Hopley owed money to was coming out to see cattle which were either collateral for a loan or had been purchased by Hopley on borrowed money. Hopley did not have the number he should have, and asked Lou if he could drive part of his (Kennedy's) herd, across the road into his (Hopley's) pasture. Both herds were Shorthorns and there was no reason the banker would suspect he was being duped. Kennedy agreed, and for a few hours his cattle grazed on Hopley grass. (The 'banker" in this instance may have been a representative of Metropolitan Life, or he may not have; the Hopley boys spread their loans around. )

Bob Kennedy has few good words for either Harry of Wayland. "They were always in debt; gave the impression of being rich, which they were, but someone was always suing them or trying to collect. It wasn't easy to get them to pay what they owed."

Elsewhere we have seen news accounts, mostly based on interviews with Peter Hopley and his sons, about the amount of grain they bought— often paying more than market price. This may have been the case with Peter. Kennedy said it was not with his sons. "They liked to buy from widows. Some farmer in the area would pass away and they'd go offer to buy his corn. Women didn't know the value of it. I know some of them didn't get paid what they should have, if anything. Women in that situation weren't likely to see a lawyer; they'd just let it go."

He gave other examples of unethical dealings. "Wayland had purebred black cattle and some high-priced bulls. Now, when you're buying calves, like a yearling bull or two, you want to see the mother cow as well. Some look good, like the kind you'd want, some don't. I can tell you that Wayland would show a buyer a good-looking cow whether she was the mother or not. He'd sell five or six yearlings that were supposedly born of the same cow the same year."

Shady deals or not, a sign of the times took place on June 22, 1933, when Harry Hopley sold his entire Shorthorn herd. The sale, held at the county fairgrounds sales pavilion, was a major event. Matt White, representing the Wallace Farmer and Iowa Homestead magazine, was there, as was F.W. Harding, Secretary of the American Shorthorn Breeders Association. One of the two auctioneers was Lt. Governor N.G. Kraschel, who was probably glad to get a couple of days away from Des Moines.

Of this event Matt White wrote: *The passing of the Hopley herd marks an epoch in Shorthorn history because it is, and has been regarded as one of the greatest herds in this country. Here is a herd that has bred its show cattle and has shown its breeding cattle, and they have been consistent winners at the various State fairs and the International during the past twenty years. . . . . I have known this herd since it was founded, and have watched its every progress until it became one of the greatest herds in this country. . . ."*

Secretary Harding went a little further, calling the Hopley herd *"one of the truly great herds of cattle on this continent. Harry Hopley deserves the keenest appreciation of his fellow breeders for the great work he has accomplished through this herd for the advancement of Shorthorn cattle".*

The sales booklet pointed out that *"parties coming from a distance will find high class accommodations at the Hotel Whitney in Atlantic."*

Why, after all those years of building the herd, sell them all? Bob Kennedy doesn't know, but he suspects creditors were pressuring Harry and he felt the need to cut back on hired labor. Tending a cow-calf operation the size of Hopley's required a lot of time and work. Bob Roush was good at feeding cattle. There was less work, therefore fewer hired men, in buying calves.

Health may also have been an issue. Harry was then fifty-two years old. While pictures taken of him at the time show a robust man who looks as if he could strap on a helmet and line up at fullback, we don't know when he began experiencing heart problems.

Harry was quoted as saying the dispersion *"is to me a sincere regret. The expansion of my steer feeding operation make it expedient for me to make this decision."*

He would fatten cattle in the future, not show and sell breeding stock.

If Harry Hopley found the dispersal a "sincere regret," he must have found the bidding dismal. Few had the kind of money Harry Hopley's purebred cattle should have been worth, and even an auctioneer who was Lt. Governor couldn't get buyers excited. A few years earlier, with cattle of no better quality, and perhaps not as good as the offering in 1933, the average price per head had been more than $1800. This sale wasn't even close.

Phil Kennedy, Bob's brother now deceased, was interested in a bargain, watched the sale closely, and kept notes. The most valuable animal offered was Browndale Goldspur, an international champion said by Will Johnson of the prestigious "Shorthorn World," to be *"The best bull and most valuable sire that can be purchased."* Of the same bull Matt White wrote: *"He is unquestionably the greatest sire of this generation."*

Browndale Goldspur went to a buyer from Colorado Springs for $1400. This was good compared to his yearling son, "Goldspur's Favorite," out of an award winning cow, who brought a meagre $125. Twelve bulls averaged only $270. Sixty cows and heifers brought an average of $133.40.

On the cover of the sales booklet Phil Kennedy wrote the words *"Harry owes us,"* and below that he has added the numbers $90.00 and $77.50 for a total of $167.50.

"Him and Wayland," Bob Kennedy repeated, "had a lot of debt."

Even so, I pointed out, it seems the Hopley family did reasonably well during tough times. Kennedy agreed. Near the end of the Depression, probably in 1939, his father was unable to make an annual payment. Foreclosure followed. The Kennedy place was then purchased by Harry and Wayland Hopley.

When Pearl Harbor was bombed Peter Hopley's sons had sold some and bought some, and still had 3,000 acres. Their cousin, Frank, retained what he'd inherited, although there wasn't as much as William had before his illness.

Tommy and George Hopley were only a year apart in age, grew up neighbors, rode the same school bus, went to classes together in Atlantic. Both were bright, good students, well-liked. Those who knew the Wayland Hopley family said George was more like his mother; perceptive, refined, an excellent student. His younger brothers were of a similar temperament as their father.

A former neighbor (Louise Hunt) recalls being in the senior class play with George. She remembers that his mother sometimes became upset with his father. Her house was immaculate and she kept it that way. She went so far as to have a large white rug. Wayland had little regard. He reportedly was prone to blustering from the feed lot to the house, storming in with boots caked in mud and manure.

George would not have done this. His younger brothers, Pete and Hickory, might have. George was soft-spoken, well behaved in school, a boy his teachers liked.

Junior (Hickory) was a seventeen-year-old bad boy when the U.S. entered World War ll. He had ability, but wasn't inclined to make the most of it. An acquaintance, who asked not to be named, said both younger brothers, even as teen-agers, had drinking binges.

Margaret Emmert, an Atlantic girl who dated and later married Pete Hopley, said her husband probably had a drinking problem while in junior high.

George and Tommy were the good kids; the heirs and anointed ones. Hickory and Pete, a classmate of the latter told me, "grew up wild."

After high school Tommy went to the state teacher's college in Wayne, Nebraska. A year later he transferred to Simpson—also primarily a teacher's college. A good many people assumed Tommy would carry on, as would George. They were young, though, might not have been sure themselves, but without doubt the opportunity was there.

The boys didn't wait for the draft. Both enlisted; George in the army, Tommy in the navy.

# Chapter Nineteen

Tommy Hopley saw his first kamikaze attack in October of 1944. His ship, the USS Luce (DD552), was not the target. The destroyer's mission at that time was to provide support for the U.S. invasion of the Philippines. While the bombardment was the heaviest the Luce had participated in to date, it was not the first. In February of that year the ship had sailed out of Attu, Alaska, joined several other destroyers in traveling about 500 miles through the frigid waters of the Bering Sea to attack the Japanese owned Kurile Islands.

The foray was a diversion—intended to draw attention from the invasion of the Marshall Island atolls—and was significant primarily because it marked the first U.S. attack of a part of the Japanese homeland. The Luce weaved through a mine field, launched a few shells onto an air field and fish cannery, ran a freighter aground, and departed without being damaged.

The Luce, a newly-built destroyer of the Fletcher class, had launched in the spring of 1943. Like others of this design, the Luce was a 21,000 ton fighting vessel, heavily armed and capable of taking a pounding. With a crew of over 350, these versatile destroyers could shoot down aircraft, launch torpedoes, find and destroy submarines, provide protection for aircraft carriers and troop transports.

Hopley, who'd been a student at Simpson College in Indianola when Pearl Harbor was bombed, enlisted two months later. Because the navy was in need of officers, Hopley was allowed to graduate, reporting for active duty in September of '43.

It was also in September of 1943 that Tommy's cousin, George, graduated from Officer's Training School at Fort Benning, Georgia.

Whether Wayland's experiences in World War l convinced him that a degree of military discipline and training would benefit his sons or, as some thought, was a good way to get the younger two out of the house, is unknown. All three, when their time came, were sent away to attend Kemper Military Academy in Booneville, Missouri.

The Kemper Academy opened in 1844 for the purpose of educating the sons (this was strictly a school for boys) of Midwest pioneers. Because students were boarded there, some came from long distances. When the founder died in 1881 his successor set about transforming the school into a military academy. A drill instructor was hired, students were required to wear grey uniforms similar to those of the U.S. Military Academy, and rigorous military discipline was enforced. By 1899 the Kemper facility was advertised as "The West Point of the West."

George Hopley led the way for his brothers, graduating from Kemper only weeks before the U.S. entered the war. He then attended the University of Iowa, served in the ROTC, and enlisted for active duty in May of 1943.

He was given a one week leave and made the most of it. Lt. Hopley spent a day with his parents at the family farm, then made a trip to West Plains, Missouri, to marry Virginia Sparks, a West Plains girl he had met at the University of Iowa. They were wed in the Methodist Church of Virginia's family on a Friday morning, took a weekend honeymoon, and arrived at West Side Farm on Tuesday, May 11. On that day Italy's unconditional surrender was announced, British forces were defeated in Burma, and Europe was not a good place for a 2nd Lieutenant to be sent. The bride had only a day to become acquainted with Helen, Wayland, Hickory and Pete. She accompanied George to Camp Breckenridge, Kentucky, from where he later shipped out for additional training and assignment. She returned to Iowa and, for a few months, lived with Wayland and Helen.

Hopley's 83rd Infantry Division arrived in England on April 16, 1944. After special training and preparation in Wales, his unit landed at Omaha Beach on June 18, just twelve days after D-Day. There followed what became known as "the hedgerow battle."

Tommy Hopley, when the hedgerow fighting began, was halfway around the world, trying to find a disabled ship in the foggy and near-freezing Bering Sea. The Luce had been given approximate co-ordinates, but electronic navigational systems were more difficult to operate, and much less reliable, than those of today. According to "DD552, Diary of a Destroyer," an excellent book by Ron Surels (Valley Graphics, Inc., published 1994) covering the ship's day-to-day activity during that period, the navigation officer, Lt. John Welsh, later related that dense clouds persisted and he went for several weeks without being able to take a single celestial reading. Hopley had been trained in sonar, primarily for submarine detection. LORAN (Long Range Navigation) was not his specialty, but both systems were located in the Combat Information Center. Hopley no doubt did what he could to help, but it wasn't much. The Luce groped about for several days. The captain fumed. Being on a disabled ship in those waters posed a significant risk, and pressure to find the missing vessel increased. After nearly two weeks of futile searching the clouds lifted, the sun rose, and it was determined the Luce had been given the wrong co-ordinates. The ship in distress was on the opposite side of the Aleutian chain.

Tom's frustration in the Bering Sea took place as his cousin was among allied forces moving toward the invasion of Germany. First, though, came a costly battle in Normandy, a fight in terrain that greatly favored defenders. Open farm fields were separated by all-but-impenetrable coastal hedges. The advance relied on tanks. Hedges were so thick tanks often hung up in the middle, or threw a track, and if they did break through the underside was riding high and exposed to anti-tank weaponry.

Infantry squads, such as the one led by Lt. George Hopley, could advance only at those narrow openings provided by tanks. The rumbling and crashing, trembling of hedges, told the Germans well in advance where those openings would be. Machine gunners had the time to set up, to focus their field of fire.

Allied engineers tried blasting the hedges, which worked to an extent but required more high explosives than were available. Saw teeth attached to the front of tanks were used. These improvised cutters proved effective and, by mid-July, as Tom Hopley and the Luce were headed for Finger Bay, Adak, for minor repairs, the 83<sup>rd</sup> advanced several miles, reaching the Lo-Perriers Road. The Normandy Campaign was ending, the next lie ahead, and the 83<sup>rd</sup> moved on.

Lt. Hopley was not with them. On Independence Day, July 4, 1944, he was killed in action. Details of his death were not made public; may not have been known. His remains arrived in Atlantic on the 20<sup>th</sup>. A memorial service was held at the Roland, Peacock & Baxter funeral home, after which burial took place at the family plot in the Oakwood Cemetery near Lewis.

There could have been a military ritual, with taps and a rifle salute that sent the sound of gunfire rolling through the evergreens bordering the cemetery, but the family requested otherwise. No weaponry, not even parade rifles, was present.

This was probably at Helen's request. While the loss devastated both parents, Wayland did not visibly fall apart. Helen did. One person who knew her searched for a way to describe Helen and settled on 'basket case;' not the most sensitive term, but the one that came to mind. Helen never got over the loss of George. She tried, however, by focusing her affections to Peter William, who was then thirteen.

Wayland and Helen memorialized the death of their son by purchasing an organ for the Atlantic Methodist Church. Nancy Hopley was not yet born, but she would become a member of that church and during her sixteen years the organ remained in use.

# Chapter Twenty

The Luce saw action as American forces took back the Philippines. From a distance crew members watched a kamikaze attack another ship. Then, in late March of 1945, she turned toward the Japanese island of Okinawa.

The war, by then, had shifted to the Allies favor. Germany had been decimated and would soon surrender. Japan was pushed back, suffering huge losses, but refused to concede. Their ground forces dug in, vowed to fight to the death, and out of the sky came their suicide planes. While these suicide bombers were not new, at Okinawa they came in waves.

Military historians tell us Japanese leaders were hopeful these tactics would cause America to accept a cessation of the conflict on terms favorable to Japan. America had no thought of this, would accept only an unconditional surrender, and the slaughter continued.

The strategy to take Okinawa had the navy implementing what was called a "flycatcher screen" to intercept suicide planes and motorboats. A flotilla of ships surrounding the island were to detect and attack, with the aid of CAP (Combat Air Patrol), incoming Japanese. Beginning on March 26, each of these stations was manned by a destroyer. Accompanying each destroyer were several small gunboats, boats sailors often referred to as "pallbearers."

The Luce was one of the destroyers placed at 30-mile intervals, patrolling night and day within 5,000 yards of her assigned position, the job to shield the land invasion from aerial attack.

The land battles for Iwo Jima, Okinawa, and Tarawa have been well publicized; the material for documentaries and movies. Losses on both sides were staggering. The valor of members of the Marines is legendary. Not so well known is the fact that hundreds of sailors lost their lives, and scores of ships went down.

The crew of the Luce was edgy but confident. Good leaders and excellent marksmen had, to that point, kept casualties and damage to a minimum. The Luce was, by Okinawa, called the "Lucky Luce." How much of a role luck played no one can say, but whatever good fortune the Luce had was soon to run out.

Within hours of reaching her battle station near the island, three Japanese aviators were spotted in the water. Two were unconscious, floating in their life jackets. The third, seeing that he was about to be taken prisoner, tried to drown himself. One of the three had attended the University of California at Berkley, returning to Japan just prior to the attack on Pearl Harbor. Disgraced by being taken prisoner, he wished to be allowed to commit suicide.

While the Luce is credited with being the first ship to fire a salvo at Okinawa, her crew expended most of their effort trying to hit flying targets. Action was fierce as Japan sent wave after wave of aircraft. The Luce shot down many, dodged torpedoes, saw other destroyers hit, damaged badly, some going to the bottom. A crew member named J.C. Phillips, SC1/c, later told of having spent days on end without going below deck. The gunners would be released to go eat, or shower, often being recalled minutes later when radar operators spotted more incoming. Ammunition would be exhausted, he wrote, and in making the short run to pick up more the Luce passed the twisted hulks of sister ships that had been blown apart, some only hours after reaching their battle posts. Phillips said that as the month of April dragged by, as days ran into nights in a blur of gun powder, deafening reports and the hum of Japanese airplanes, he reached the point at which he knew it was not if the Luce would be hit, it was when.

One of the ship's many battle reports describes how, just before sunset on April 13, enemy aircraft approached from the southwest. They were fired on and turned back. Less than an hour later a plane came in low making a torpedo run off the starboard beam. The five inch battery opened fire at 8,000 yards. At 3,500 yards the 40 mm guns opened up. The plane, flying at full throttle, came on. The Luce turned toward the aircraft to present as small a target as possible, guns blazing away. The torpedo was launched and then, at 1,600 yards, the plane was hit and nosedived into the sea. The torpedo narrowly missed, passed just astern, and water erupted in a violent explosion that occurred when the torpedo reached the end of its run.

A Kamikaze was shot down at 1,500 yards a short time later, burned in the water for an estimated 15 minutes before sinking. Another torpedo plane followed, then a dive bomber, each disintegrating in the gamut of gunfire. Lt. Cliff Jones recounted how a plane flown by a Korean pilot was shot down. The pilot survived and was thrown a line. He would tell, through an interpreter, that he was a farmer who had been taken into custody by Japanese, given a few flying lessons and his orders. He was told a bomb attached to his plane would detonate if he tried to land. Above him and other Kamikaze pilots were Japanese fighters who would shoot down any who tried to defect.

Through all of this Tommy Hopley was in the ship's Command Information Center (CIC). He was no doubt as stressed and exhausted as his comrades. Hopley, trained by the Navy in electronics, was among those monitoring the screens, watching for blips, making calls to notify gunners and friendly aircraft. The ship's doctor, Lt. Shaffner, called the CIC "very active," occupied by men running on adrenalin, men fully aware of how near to death they might be.

Days passed. Stories circulated of ships and men being maimed and killed by the seeming non-stop barrage of kamikazes. There was no questioning these accounts—crew members could see and hear the carnage going on around them.

Fear and dread of these planes and the determined, suicidal pilots who flew them grew with each encounter. None aboard the Luce could relate to the intense commitment the enemy had to kill themselves in a failed cause. Some, like the Korean pilot, felt they had no choice. But others, including those Japanese pilots brought aboard early in the encounter, were anxious to end their lives—preferably taking American with them—but intent on suicide regardless.

A sailor named Walter Fisher expressed the sentiments of many aboard the Luce. In the last letter he would send to his wife he wrote that he realized, more forcibly than ever, what it was he was fighting for. "I hope," he concluded, "I live through it all to profit from its lessons."

He and Tom Hopley died the same day, probably within minutes of each other.

May 4 dawned clear and bright; a sunrise that was not a welcome sight on the Luce. Cloud cover and stormy weather grounded the dreaded air attacks. This day was ideal for flying.

Early that morning, while some who had been on night watch were starting breakfast, technicians in CIC spotted bogies, many of them, at 60 miles and closing. CIC reported that ships at other picket stations were under attack. General Quarters, signaled by the ear-splitting "bong-bong-bong" of the G.Q. horn, was sounded.

Tom Blanck, yeoman first class, had been up all night. He remembered that raids had been steady on the previous day, sporadic but frequent for weeks. The crew was bone-weary, punchy, "dead," in his words, "on their feet."

"I heard that 90 planes were coming toward us. Our fighter planes were directed to them and followed them all the way, picking them off. They were knocking the heck out of them all the way in, but it was such a huge raid that some broke through. They always did. . . . "

Norman Foreman, a 20 mm gunner, looked from a hatchway at numerous airplanes. He suddenly realized they were not ours. He dashed to his gun, and cocked the big weapon. Doing so was no small feat. The 22 mm was cocked by two men; one couldn't do it. Foreman observed that "when you're scared enough you can," and he did.

Two planes peeled from the formation and zeroed in on the Luce. More followed. "Twenty-eight bogies!" gunners heard on their earphones, "Twenty-eight bogies!"

The first plane came fast, from an angle that prevented guns being brought to bear. The captain ordered a hard rudder. A 20 mm gunner described the plane as a bomber, coming off the port bow in a steep dive. The anti-aircraft gun had stops, limiting where it could be pointed, to assure the ship did not shoot itself. When the plane finally appeared in the gun sights it was so close the rivets were visible. A man on the bridge said he saw a smile on the pilot's face. The plane veered sharply to avoid a string of fire, then turned again, taking hits but still flying.

Men on the bridge fell face down, sure impact was imminent. The tail section was blasted from the bomber, perhaps causing it to narrowly miss the bridge, and it screamed just above the Luce and crashed into the sea. The impact was so close that, when the suicide bomb detonated, power on the Luce was knocked out. Some crew members were injured by shrapnel. Several others were killed. Many who were there believe that bomb, which exploded about 30 yards from the Luce, opened a seam below the water line.

Another plane followed seconds later, this time from the port side, and, with the electrical system partially down, the Luce lost some ability to maneuver. The plane was riddled with shells, kept coming and suddenly another joined it. Both struck the Luce, impact coming so close together survivors heard only one explosion. Some reports have a third plane striking mid-ship on the port side—events were happening too fast—and those who might have seen the third plane were killed. One bomb penetrated to the Luce's magazine and a tremendous explosion followed. The deck was littered with the gore of mutilated bodies and badly injured crewmen. The Luce's guns, those not disabled, fired away; at times narrowly missing our own planes. Japanese planes were driven back, but only for a few minutes. The Luce was a sitting duck, listing, leaking like a sieve.

Probably less than five minutes elapsed between the first kamikaze strike and the last, and a few minutes later the stern was sinking, bow rising. The ship went vertical, headed stern first for the bottom.

Men in engine and control rooms below deck called their question up to the bridge: was the ship sinking? Should they abandon their stations? Initially the captain, not yet knowing the extent of damage, ordered them to "stand fast." They did, and never had a chance.

The order to abandon came moments later, although with much of the electrical system not working many did not hear it. Some put life jackets on injured comrades and pushed them overboard. One survivor remembers seeing money; lots of money. Payday was at hand and one of the explosions had apparently scattered contents of the safe.

One of the enlisted men in the Combat Information Center was Tom Matisak. Years later, while being interviewed by Ron Surels for his book on the Luce, he said he and Lt. John Hutchinson spent anxious moments waiting for instructions. One of them, using a voice tube connected to the bridge because other communications systems were out, had asked for directions, for an indication of how badly the Luce was damaged. Matisak, feeling the ship moving in a way it should not have, was hoping someone would give the order to abandon. He looked around, he said, and made a decision—if even one officer made a move to leave he'd be right behind him. Seconds later Lt. Hutchinson headed for the hatch.

On his way out Matisak glanced back. He saw a man he'd worked with for weeks, Lt. JG Tommy Hopley. Hopley was still at his post, struggling with a mass of phone lines and wires that had apparently fallen from overhead as a result of explosions. The wires were entangled with his kapok life preserver. Another enlisted man, a radio operator named Murzycki, also saw Hopley. Murzycki said he thought Hopley had freed himself, but no one can say with certainty. Four officers in the CIC perished. None of the survivors knew if Hopley went to the bottom in the control room, or escaped it to die elsewhere.

335 seamen were aboard the Luce that day. Nearly half were either killed outright or reported as missing in action, a status that changed a few days later to presumed dead. Rescue came, for most survivors, within two hours. Sharks, however, arrived sooner. An unknown number of men, probably only a few, survived the kamikazes, separated themselves from the ship, then were butchered by sharks.

Of the two Hopley boys, assumed to be eventual heirs to the farming operations began by Peter and William, one was in Oakwood Cemetery, the other buried at sea.

# Chapter Twenty-One

The end of the Great Depression might have marked a new beginning for Hopley Farms. With better economic times, however, came war. While the worst blow was the death of two young men—boys who might have returned with maturity, a measure of wisdom, and an appreciation for life and opportunity—there were other problems as well.

Wayland, in his late forties when Pearl Harbor was bombed, had his debts and short-term set-backs but the basis of Hopley wealth—land—had been nearly all retained. While George was gone, Hickory (Wayland, Jr.) turned seventeen, old enough in years to accept responsibility. Pete (Peter William) was ten when George was born. Their grandfather, at the same age, knew what work was.

Harry, on West Side Farm, had his sixtieth birthday in 1941. He was not in good health and, other than his wife and a niece they'd raised but not adopted, had no heirs. He and Wayland were close, partners on some operations, and a likely eventuality was that one day Wayland and sons would acquire Harry's land and combine the two operations.

While this would partially take place, "Wayland Hopley and Sons" was never a flourishing operation.

Harry was Peter's oldest son and filled the expected role, and Wayland had achievements of his own. He was prominent in cattlemen's organizations and committees and county groups doing work that potentially had a direct impact on his operation. He is recognized for his long-term association with the development of Black Angus cattle, served as president of the Iowa Beef Producer's Association, and held other similar posts. Although he did not run for public office, he served on numerous boards and committees on the county, state, and national level. He associated with people like Harry Swan.

Swan, who had a lot in common with Wayland Hopley, was born in Atlantic in 1894 (the same year as Wayland), took part-time jobs as a boy, saved his money, attended college (Swan worked his way through, Wayland did not) served in WW1 (as did Wayland), then returned to Atlantic to practice law—and politics. He knew, and may have been influenced by, Col. Kraschel. Swan ran for the office of Iowa Attorney General in 1934. He lost, but made an impression. Five years later he was elected chair of the state Republican Party. Republicans leaders on the national level searched for a way to defeat the seemingly perennial president—Franklin Roosevelt—and Harry Swan attracted their attention. Making a name for himself in Iowa, Swan was considered a viable candidate for the leadership of the Republican National Party. Then, in 1941, driving too fast on narrow Highway 6 to attend a meeting in Des Moines, his car spun out of control. Swan was dead at the scene.

His funeral was among the largest Atlantic has ever seen. Iowa's governor (Bourke Hickenlooper) delivered an address. Pallbearers included a former governor, a U.S. Congressman, and Wayland Hopley.

Hopley worked with Harry Swan on issues other than those having to do with agriculture and electing Republicans. Chet Woodward had been a neighbor when Wayland was a boy growing up in the Hopley Mansion in Lewis. Woodward and his family created the Crystal Lake amusement park when Wayland was a toddler, and over the years he spent countless hours there. By the 1930s, with Chet grown old, there was a movement to make the place a state park. Wayland Hopley joined the cause. The state initially balked. A group of Lewis residents, including Wayland Hopley, persuaded Harry Swan to get involved. Swan was well-connected at the state capital. Not long after Swan signed on, the state Conservation Commission changed their position. They would make Crystal Lake a state park if the land was given to them. Woodward offered a bargain price, Hopley donated, and he served on a committee that raised more.

Although Crystal Lake (Cold Springs State Park) was one of several projects Wayland Hopley and Harry Swan had a part in, Hopley's best years, in terms of political influence, came after both his brother and Swan were dead.

Federal agencies sought his advice on food rationing programs. He made numerous trips to Washington, appeared before Congressional committees, and when he had an opinion he did not hold back.

One of the wartime agencies created by the Roosevelt Administration was the Office of Price Administration (OPA). The OPA was given the authority to set prices—and subsidies—for certain commodities. Their goal was to see that the armed forces first and, secondly, the private sector, received necessities without price gouging. Ideally, producers would make a reasonable profit and consumers, including the Defense Department (for the military), would pay a reasonable price.

In Wayland Hopley's estimation, cattle feeders got pinched. Beef and pork was rationed and hard to get, yet feedlots were far from capacity. Hopley was anxious to let the public know why. The *Lincoln Journal* was among numerous Corn Belt newspapers that sent a reporter.

*Atlantic, Ia.—Right here on these 1,450 acres of rich western Iowa land that Wayland Hopley farms, you get the reason for empty butcher shops. Normally—and that means for ten years past—Wayland Hopley would have fattened on his pastures and in his feed lots from 750 to 1,000 western cattle. Today, as we talk on the cool front porch of the Hopley farmhouse he has 140 cattle left out of the 350 he finished this year.*

*Wayland's brother, Harry, who usually feeds out from 1,500 to 1,600 prime cattle, will market 400 this year. George Gross, four miles west of the Hopley farm, who produces in normal years 2,000 fat steers and heifers, will send less than half that number or less. (Lincoln Journal, June 22, 1945)*

The article goes on to quote Hopley as saying the OPA had allowed the price of corn to increase by 33%, protein feeds by 200-300%. Hopley said he raised about 40,000 bushel of corn per year, but bought an additional 80,000, plus a lot of protein. Hopley then laid out the system of bureaucratic regulations that provided subsidies here, subsidies there, price controls on feeder calves, as well as fat cattle, with the end result being a net loss for every slaughter-ready steer produced.

When Hopley said he'd given a lot for the war effort there could be no doubt—he'd given his oldest son. Now he was asked to feed cattle at a loss because the government gave him no choice. He did, however, have a choice regarding how many he would produce. He said he was among stockmen nationwide who had cut back for that reason, and until the OPA figured this out beef would continue to be in short supply.

Government price-fixing of cattle, Hopley added, did not take into account the increased labor cost of production, and herein was another problem.

Farming 1,450 acres (this did not include pasture land) with horses and two-row equipment of the 1930s took more than a few good men. Most of these men were in the armed forces. Women joined the workforce in unprecedented numbers, but they were more inclined to find employment in stores and factories. Not many women became farmhands. Farmers on an eighty or 160 acre place could often manage without hired help. Larger operations could not.

Federal officials, even as the labor shortage grew more acute, were dealing with the problem of prisoners-of-war. Mostly Germans, these former enemy soldiers were arriving in this country by the thousands. Placing them in medium-security facilities was an option—an expensive one—so how about sending them off to work?

In southwest Iowa a POW camp was established in Clarinda. Administrators of this camp made them available—for a price. The rate was 50 cents per hour per prisoner, plus room and board. Wages went to the government administrator to be paid to prisoners (who received the regular monthly military salary they would have gotten if still in the German army, plus 80c per day). Cass County established a prisoner of war commission necessary to screen applicants and place prisoners. A number of POW laborers went to the county poor farm, others to area farmers and still others to various commercial entities with a need. Wayland Hopley applied for ten prisoners, and got them. Harry Hopley did likewise. Both, at the time, said if the POWs worked out, they'd employ more. This didn't happen.

Wayland would later, on a trip to the nation's capital to offer testimony and advice to a Congressional committee on food rationing, venture into another subject. POW labor was, in his view, worse than none. He'd modified his horse barn to provide suitable quarters, fed the men well, but they were not good workers. He found them sullen, lazy, untrustworthy. If he or a foreman provided direct supervision they would at least go through the motions. Left on their own they quit, took a nap, or otherwise amused themselves.

The shortage of farm labor, Hopley stressed, was a major problem. German prisoners were, in his experience, not the answer. (Atlantic News Telegraph, Sept. 29, 1944)

Harry Hopley had also spent money on bars and locks needed to meet requirements associated with housing summer-time prisoner-workers, and ended up with little to show for it other than a few medium-security horse stalls. Harry, though, was lacking more than reliable labor. He needed management. His heart condition was getting worse. A man who had once ran kick-offs back 100 yards, played both offense and defense for the Atlantic Maroons, wrestled steers, broke horses and hand-picked 100 bushels of corn a day, found himself light-headed and short of breath following activities that had once been routine. His heart was not doing the job it once had. Doctors of the 1940s had limited options. Harry took his pills and tried to avoid exertion. Managing more than 1,200 acres, including row crops and hayfields, with several hundred cattle and hogs on feed, with a constant shortage of labor—reliable or otherwise—took a toll. 1944 saw a rapid decline in his health. Early that year he was bedfast for several weeks. He and Della, before the summer was over, reached a decision they'd contemplated for some time.

The News Telegraph carried the story in January of 1945.

*Because of ill health and a shortage of labor, Harry Hopley, prominent Atlantic cattleman, has leased all his farming land— some 1,200 acres—at his place southwest of here, retaining only pasture land to carry on his feeding business. Leasing the land are W.L. Ferrell and his brothers, all of whom have been farming in the Colfax vicinity.*

*W.L. Ferrell and his family have moved to the Hopley place and his brothers will locate there in the early spring.*

*Mr. Hopley, who has suffered from a heart ailment for several years, has been confined to his bed for the past month.*

*He is one of the best-known cattlemen in the Midwest and for
many years was engaged with his father, the late Peter Hopley,
in the importation of blooded horses.*

*The Hopley family first came to Cass County in 1866,
where they were engaged in farming and livestock. Another
son, Wayland A. Hopley, is also a widely known stockman and
breeder of pure bred Angus at his ranch southwest of Atlantic.*

(The reference to the family arriving in 1866 is worth noting, as
this error appears in repeated newspaper articles. Census records and
other reliable sources clearly show Thomas and Francis and children
coming to Cass County in 1857, although an older son may have made
the trip a few months earlier. One of the several histories of Cass
County erroneously put the date at 1866, and many writers since then
have repeated the mistake.)

In February, a month after the lease arrangement was announced,
Harry underwent heart surgery in Omaha Methodist. A few days later
he was back at West Side Farm, occupying the house he had all-but
completely rebuilt for Della shortly before their wedding. He was there
for only a few months. By late summer it was apparent the surgery
had been of no lasting benefit. He and Della, in early October, rented a
home in Omaha in order to be near his doctor and the hospital.

His thoughts as he left West Side Farm for the last time were not
recorded. He was a realist, though, and must have considered the
possibility that he might not return. (By contrast, his younger brother
drove out of the same driveway twenty years later with every expectation
of being back in an hour or so.)

Pneumonia hospitalized Harry shortly after he and Della settled into
their new home in Omaha. This was followed by another heart attack,
and in mid-November he was dead.

Another funeral, another estate. This, like many prior to it, was not
easy. There were a number of minor claims, those totaling less than
$1500. There were also a couple of larger ones. Back when Peter died in
1926 a sister, Minnie Hopley Muffley, was apparently owed $30,000 for
her share of her parent's estate. The note, due in ten years and carrying
5% interest had, according to Minnie, been lost. A similar amount

($33,175.60) was claimed on behalf of another sister, Edna (deceased), by her son and heir, Peter Askew. (As has previously been noted, Peter Hopley—following the death of his wife—did considerable planning for the distribution of his estate. He wanted as much as possible to go to his heirs; giving Margaret the house in Lewis, making similar arrangements with other children on other holdings, and so on. The declared value of his real estate at the time of his death was just $19,000, and other assets a meager few thousand more. This, of course, was all but absurd—the man was worth well over a million dollars. He felt no reluctance to circumvent tax laws and, as his sons might have put it, "screwing the government." He wanted his children to have it, and have it in equitable shares. Because of real estate and horse and cattle arrangements just what was fair was debatable. For some, compensation was to be made in cash—thus the amount owed to Edna and Minnie. The brothers evidently didn't have the cash on hand, so notes were issued. The Great Depression followed, and those obligations remained outstanding.)

These notes—assuming them to be legitimate—were not entirely Harry's liability. The brothers had gotten much of Peter's farmland, crops, livestock and related assets; Wayland owed his share, which may have been larger than Harry's. The distribution, though, of Harry's estate afforded an opportunity for claims to be filed.

As lawyers worked through this snarl, Della remained in Omaha. Eleanor had married and was living there, and Della apparently preferred being in the city and close to the niece she had raised as a daughter. There were other issues. All the land held by Harry and Della was, shortly after his death, transferred to her name. Wayland's attorney, apparently to protect his interests, initiated legal action blocking the transfer until certain unspecified issues were resolved.

Della, in 1946, sold the house on West Side Farm, along with outbuildings and most of the farmland, to Wayland. He and Helen moved there, while young Hickory—recently married to Shirley Powers—moved into the home Wayland had built for Helen.

Della held title to some of what had been West Side Farm until her death, at which time she left the estate to Eleanor Forsythe Liston.

With the war ended, Wayland Hopley's trips to Washington declined, as did any influence he might have had there, but he remained involved in local affairs. His brother was frequently asked to speak at club or fraternal meetings, to serve as toastmaster or master of ceremonies, and did so in a satisfactory manner. With him gone, these invitations tended to go to Wayland. He was probably more entertaining. Wayland was not as handsome or imposing as the once-athletic Harry had been. He didn't try to be. On the farm he dressed like a farmer, cursed, spit, chewed a tired cigar, and scratched himself where he itched. But he knew how to clean up. He had expensive suits, $5 neckties and cuff links. He'd been to Washington. He could comment with insight on political issues, had a down-to-earth way of expressing himself, and he could tell jokes—clean and otherwise. There was an edge of crudeness to Wayland; he wasn't going to take the podium and say something outlandish, but on the other hand one could never be completely sure.

The disastrous Main Street fire of 1948 wiped out a good share the Lewis business district. Wayland Hopley was not an owner of any of these business places, but he was among a group of Lewis area residents who committed to rebuild. He donated money and helped raise more. A "Memorial Building," a 40 foot by 100 foot Quonset was suggested; a structure with a full basement, the aggregate offering ample space to serve as the center of Lewis community activities. While Wayland Hopley was just one of many who contributed and organized, he was well-known and vocal and was recognized for his participation when the dedication program was planned. The following appeared in the Atlantic News Telegraph on October 4, 1949:

> *Citizens of Lewis will celebrate the community's recovery from the fire of June, 1948, at a special dedication of the Lewis Memorial Building at 8 p.m. tonight. Main address will be by Roscoe Jones, Atlantic attorney, and Wayland Hopley will serve as master of ceremonies. Included in the entertainment will be musical numbers by Lewis school students.*
>
> *The Memorial Building, to be used for community gatherings and public programs, is a Quonset type with a brick front. Yet to be installed is the $1700 automatic gas heating plant, donated by the War Veterans of the community.*
>
> *Lete King served as chairman of the building committee.*

*The dedication of the Memorial Building climaxes a project which replaced a number of structures destroyed by the 1948 fire.*

Roscoe Jones was Wayland Hopley's attorney.

We were unable to locate any former students of the Lewis school who remember singing at the dedication, but there are probably a few still around. The designation "Memorial Building" was short-lived. The structure became known as the Community Building, later the Activity Center, and today most of the space is used for the storage of a strange collection of thousands of owl replicas.

Wayland graduated from high school in Lewis, and hIs personal loyalty was in that town. It was probably Helen who chose to send their sons to Atlantic.

A few days before the dedication ceremony in Lewis, Wayland and Helen made a trip to Booneville, Missouri. They went to take their son, Pete, to Kemper Military Academy. Hickory had spent time there, and Pete would do so as well. We don't know what prompted the parents to make this decision. Wayland's service in World War1 might have caused him to feel a taste of military life would do the boys good. Perhaps they were thinking of George and his military training. People who knew the family suspected there may have been other reasons. The boys needed discipline and weren't getting it, or at least submitting, at home. They were often out-of-control. Both, even while in high school, were said to have drinking binges. One lady we spoke with, who asked that her name not be connected with the allegation, said she knew the family well and believed the boys were sent to boarding school at Kemper Academy just to get them out of the house. They were not, in her view, easy to deal with—particularly after the death of George.

Whether Kemper Academy was beneficial to Hickory and Pete (and their subsequent life would indicate it was not), the next few years were good ones for Wayland and Helen. Labor was plentiful, cattle prices were generally favorable, hogs made a reliable profit.

Wayland sold some land in the 1940s—a quarter section plus fifty acres to Donald Ray, a few acres to the county for a road, a couple of hundred to the Johnson family (Metro Life held a mortgage on this land, which was paid off as a result). A deal that took shape in the 1940s, probably a subject of discussion at the Okoboji vacation, was finalized in 1950. Walnut Grove feed company bought fifty acres of Hopley land for a research farm, with an additional tract to Walnut Grove for residential building lots that became the luxurious home of the company president.

Wayland and Helen also bought some—1,200 acres from Della (Harry's estate) in 1946. They also purchased what had been Frank Miller's farm, and acquired ownership of long-abandoned railroad right-of-way. Newspaper accounts of the time (Council Bluffs Nonpareil, Nov. 6, 1946) put his holdings in land at 3,000 acres; about the same as the combined amount the brothers owned before the Depression. What he sold over the next few years was probably, at least in part, a consolidation for the purpose of paying debts that may have dated to previous estate claims. Plats of the mid-1950s show Wayland still in ownership of more than 1700 contiguous acres.

Pete and Margaret Emmert met and dated in high school. Despite her parental disapproval, they were married In 1953. Margaret, daughter of the president of the Atlantic State Bank, might have had some premonition on her honeymoon that Pete wasn't to be the ideal husband. The couple drove first to Wayland and Helen's Okoboji lake home, then traveled on to Las Vegas. They checked into a hotel/casino. Pete left Margaret to unpack and settle in, saying he was going to "look around." He found whiskey and gambling and returned the next day.

Wayland's Angus show-stock won consistently. Margaret recalls traveling with Wayland and Helen and, sometimes, Hickory, to the national livestock show in Denver, as well as making several trips to Chicago with rail cars of fat cattle. The women shopped at fine stores, spent lavishly, and all stayed at the famous Palmer House; Chicago's most noted luxury hotel. Shirley did not make these trips. Margaret told us that Hickory was a dedicated woman-chaser and, in her estimation, having his wife along would have been an impediment.

The Hopley annual sale was part party—part business. Wayland liked to entertain, especially if there was profit incentive, and Helen seems to have enjoyed being hostess. The sales were not a new event, but in the post-war years they evolved.

Previously—during the 19-teens, 20s and 30s—held at the depot stockyards or fairgrounds or the Goeken's renovated barn, the site shifted after Harry's death to the West Side Farm. Earlier sales had, following completion, been celebrated by a banquet at one of Atlantic's hotel dining rooms. The guest list was limited to buyers, auctioneers, and others who helped make the sale a success. Liquor flowed at these post-sales parties. Wayland recognized that a bit of pre-sale booze might have a tendency to loosen up buyers. There were those attending sales of Hopley purebred stock that never touched a drop, but it wasn't for lack of opportunity. Wayland and Helen, at what was usually a two-to-three day event, prepared by buying liquor by the case. Beer was on ice, and on the evening before the sale potential buyers were treated to a gala barbeque. Johnny's Restaurant, near the Omaha stockyards, was considered to be one of that city's finest. They often were retained to cater the barbeque. Ribs and steaks and side dishes and all the fine spirits buyers cared to consume, free of charge, put them in a mood to bid and brought them back year after year.

While Wayland and his wife presided over these events., they were cautious drinkers (particularly Helen, who drank very little). Wayland liked his bourbon and scotch, but generally in moderation. Those we interviewed who remember say he either held his liquor well or watched his consumption. He was the host, he presided, he was in control. His surviving sons, these same people told us, drank with abandon and were more likely to become obnoxious as not.

When Helen and Wayland had their grand parties, he must have recalled those hosted by his parents; or just Edna. His mother's idea of a card party was thirty to fifty ladies, a multi-course luncheon, and an afternoon during which those between games strolled through the garden or admired Edna's selections in art and furnishings.

While Helen and Wayland hosted and enjoyed pre-sale parties attended by several hundred, their preferred entertainment was to be half a foursome in a quiet evening of canasta. She liked the game and he learned to play. Once a week, if arrangements could be made, they played with Harold and Cornelia (Corny) Schrauger or one of two or three other couples that were more or less regulars.

They owned their summer home on Spirit Lake until Helen sold it after her husband's death. Grandchildren remember Helen and Wayland fondly—he gruff yet funny, with the ever-present cigar and a vocabulary that included exciting new words—she as warm and matronly, often wearing a full apron and cooking pastries for children at the summer home and big noon meals on the farm. Helen made fruitcake, said to be well laced with brandy. Her granddaughter, Pam, was fascinated by Helen's jewelry. She remembers Helen dressing in custom-made suits for card parties and family events, and grandchildren remember a lady who always found the time to talk when the youngsters wanted to.

# Chapter Twenty-Two

Wayland, after Harry's death, achieved a status that set him apart from anyone else in his immediate family—past, present or future. Peter, of course, had been the founding father—the man who made a million and fought Indians and told an ever-interested media how he did it. He, however, shared the stage with William. Peter became wealthier, had the more colorful life, was more sought by the press. Still, William did quite well. William had a livelier and more imaginative sense of humor than Peter. Both qualified as Cass County pioneers, and were respected as such.

By the time William died, Harry was well-established. For years it was Peter and William, then Peter and Harry. This evolved to Harry and Wayland, with Harry the big brother and senior partner. Following Harry's death there was not another influential Hopley in Cass County. Cousin Frank was living, but hardly a factor. Frank turned seventy shortly after his only son was killed on the Luce. He had sold out in South Dakota and returned to the home place in Cass County, held things together through the Depression, retaining what remained of William's holdings. But with Tommy gone William's place would pass to someone outside the family. Frank retired within months of learning Tommy's fate. He and his wife moved to Atlantic, where she died in 1946 and he a few years later.

Wayland was, in the late 1940s, through the 1950s and into the 60s, the go-to Hopley. When a newspaper or magazine wanted a quote from a representative of the well-known family, there was only Wayland.

Wayland, Jr.—Hickory—was relegated to the back seat. As time passed, it seemed that's where he belonged. He and Shirley got along for a few years. They had children, he farmed and fed cattle with his father, went to stock shows, but he was never really a partner in the way Harry and is father had been.

An argument could be made that Wayland enjoyed his position, wasn't anxious to share with Junior. Most of those we interviewed felt Hickory deserved no better. They knew him as an irresponsible drinker and womanizer, a man who threw away money and opportunities.

Regardless of why, Hickory drifted in and out of Wayland's operation and tried various other endeavors. Each of these had several things in common: Hickory was not inclined to work for someone else. He was in charge. He also chose a succession of businesses he knew nothing about.

All were financed with backing from Wayland. And, one by one, they all failed.

Some family members have said the downfall began with the Depression, and was sealed with the deaths of George and Tommy. The Depression was unquestionably bad. Net farm worth plummeted, debts were accumulated, some land was sold.

Family folklore has it that Wayland loaned money to destitute neighbors and was never repaid. His estate settlement shows there was continued reliance on loans—big ones—from Metropolitan Life. Both Harry and Wayland, however, emerged from the Depression with title to roughly as much land as they had going in (the 500 acres south of Marne was sold, but the Kennedy farm was added).

Frank Hopley, Hickory's son, said that when the time came for his father to take over he simply wasn't prepared. Young Pete said the same of his father.

While this is no doubt true, the fact is that nearly twenty years passed between the death of George and that of Wayland. At the time of George's memorial service his younger brothers knew the day would come. George was out of the picture. Someday either Hickory or Pete—or both—would take over Hopley Farms. They had two decades to prepare.

Young Pete, in reminiscing about his grandparents, was struck by the fact that he could not recall ever seeing Wayland perform physical labor. He was a manager. Wayland was out and about day after day, wearing wash pants and a buttoned shirt, teeth clamped on an unlit cigar, barking out orders. His boots might be caked with mud and manure, but his hands were usually clean.

Frank, who worked construction while still in high school and went on to found and manage a successful business in Chicago, only shrugged when I mentioned this. He saw his grandfather as an overseer. His time was better spent in that capacity than physical labor, but both were of equal importance.

These somewhat different views bring to mind Peter Hopley. Peter repeatedly wrote and spoke of years of sun-up to sun-down labor. No couple, he boasted, had ever worked harder than he and Edna. Doing so, starting with nothing and turning it into value, built character. Wayland did not have the same experience. Harry, the oldest son, spent days on the farm with his father. He was also primarily a manager, but in his youth was part of the labor force. He had his own farm, taking care of the home place when Peter traveled and Wayland at first too young, then away. Peter's youngest son was born a manager, whether this was his strong point or not. He went to college, then to war. When Wayland returned from France in 1919 his future was secure. He and his bride would move into the house that was finished while he was overseas and he would assume his role as co-manager of his father's farms.

Peter Hopley (the original), even in old age, worked with his hands. As an old man he did not overdo it, but he went through the motions. When he saw a minor fencing repair that needed attention he was apt to fix it himself. After his fortune was made and he took a team and wagon to the field and picked corn he was there for the show and the nostalgia. He did not pick fifty bushel and scoop it into the crib as he once had. He tossed a few ears, then turned the job over to a hired man.

Whether this trait impressed employees we don't know, but he was telling them he understood, he identified with what they did. Labor was not, even in old age and wealth, beneath him.

Wayland was not one to mix managing with physical work, and his sons took note.

The boy who was christened Wayland lll later became known as Frank Hopley (he did not legally change his name, as some have said, just let it be known he preferred "Frank"). He was born in 1947 (100 years after Peter and three years after George was killed), and said he felt the death of the oldest son changed family dynamics. He agreed with those who maintain George had been much like, and close to, his mother. He was her favorite. With his death this affection transferred to Pete. She doted on him, according to Frank, and spoiled him.

Frank remembers Pete (his uncle) as being a fun guy, gregarious and popular with girls. He drove a sporty car. If he felt like working he did, but this urge did not often strike. There were no consequences for bad behavior. Kemper Military Academy seems to have had no better success than the parents in instilling discipline or self-control in either boy. Pete was kicked out of Kemper. Hickory dropped out of Iowa State University.

Hickory looked and behaved, Frank said, more like his father. Wayland and Hickory related. So, in their own way, did Helen and Pete.

While Hickory farmed for a few years with his father, the relationship was strained. Frank, recalling things he was told by his parents, offered the example of a cattle deal in which his father and the senior Wayland went into partnership and made money. The profit remained, though, with Wayland. When their joint ventures were successful, it was Wayland who gained. When these ventures failed, in Frank's view, Hickory was blamed. There was also a conflict between Helen and Hickory's wife. Hickory was nineteen when he married Shirley Powers in 1944. Shortly thereafter they moved into the house on the old White Pole Road— the home built for Helen at the time of her marriage. Frank says his mother was a slovenly housekeeper. He told of stacks of dirty dishes, of rummaging through piles of clothing to find a comparatively clean shirt. Shirley just didn't do household chores. Hickory didn't seem to mind. Helen, an immaculate housekeeper, did. She was particularly distressed to see the condition of the home in which she began her marriage and spent—up until that time—most of her life.

With their farming relationship not going well, Hickory asked his father for financial backing in a string of business ventures opened between the mid-1950s and Wayland's death in 1965. One was a wholesale tire and hardware business in Atlantic. Another was a rodeo, undertaken a short time after opening the truck stop and restaurant called Hopco's. Wayland stopped short of telling tell his son no, although with some of this he must have had doubts.

Highway 6 carried a lot of truck traffic, but there were obvious problems. The location chosen was on Hopley land, near where the railroad siding had been. Four miles to the west was an existing truck stop; one established years before. Five miles north was Atlantic, with service stations and motels and restaurants galore. If that wasn't enough, the Interstate highway system was coming and most everyone knew it. Even if Hickory had been able to prevail over local competition, Interstate 80 meant truck traffic on Highway 6 was going to dry up.

A number of roadside restaurants and service stations on Highway 6, and other east-west routes across Iowa, were offered for sale during the 1950s as President Eisenhower advanced his plan for an Interstate highway system. Hickory's timing in opening a new one could have hardly have been worse.

Frank believes Wayland used money to control his son. He wanted Hickory close, but not too close. Hickory lacked the incentive to strike off on his own. He was dependent on his father's financing. If the two couldn't reach an agreement on farming together, he'd try other ventures. Always, though, these were underwritten by Wayland.

The question as to what extent alcohol was an issue with Hickory is one that draws varied answers. Frank and his sister, Susan Kesterson, say their father hardly drank. Susan remembers sundown rides with her father, watching the leaves turn and taking in the serenity of the countryside. Frank generally agrees; his Uncle Pete was the hard drinker, not his father.

Ellie Rutherford is one of those who recalls a different Hickory Hopley.

Among his misadventures were several involving the rodeo. He reached the point at which he lost interest in the day-to-day management of a truck stop that was bleeding money. A rodeo offered new promise, new excitement.

Even though Wayland fretted, spent more time at Hopco's doing things Hickory should have been, told an employee he sincerely wished he'd have dropped his namesake off a river bridge while still a baby, he co-signed another note. A rodeo arena, small but complete with corrals and chutes and grandstands and an announcer's box, was built. A rodeo takes livestock—roping steers, bulls, bucking and roping horses. Hickory, with more of Wayland's money on the line, bought an assortment of animals, some of them costlier than Wayland's purebred Angus cattle. He made the stock available to other rodeos. In this manner, during the late 1950s and early 60s, Hickory toured the Midwest.

He actually had a rodeo with quality animals and prize money sufficient to attract cowboys who competed on the Midwest circuit, and the first year or two were promising.

Ellie Rutherford and her husband worked for Hickory Hopley. They drove trucks transporting stock and, after arrival, had other jobs. One of hers was collecting the entry fee charged to competitors. This was usually paid in cash. By the time each performance started she would have a sizeable amount of money, which she turned over to Hickory. Ellie said Hickory's reputation for night life and womanizing was earned. He went from bar to bar, drinking and buying. Ellie said her boss often showed up the next day hung over and broke. This happened to the extent that a sober Hickory finally instructed Mrs. Rutherford to stop giving him money. If he asked she was to say no. Hide it. Keep it until the engagement was over and the outfit was headed home.

Frank, as a teenager, went along on a few rodeos. He saw a Hickory who was all business and was, at most, an occasional social drinker.

# Chapter Twenty-Three

By 1960, with Wayland reaching social security eligibility, Hickory's marriage had fallen apart. He had girlfriends and made little effort to hide the fact. Pete, back in Iowa with the buddies he grew up with, spent too much time drinking with them. As an auctioneer he was not a Col. Kraschel. He was accustomed to the good life, regardless of his income. Margaret also enjoyed living well. She, however, had a set of values she wanted to instill in her children—through example. Her husband was not the role model she had hoped for.

Pete could be contrite, thoughtful; a considerate and caring husband and father. Then would come a binge of gambling and drinking and losing money, episodes that didn't abate as he grew older. A sloppy drunk, he could go from funny to obnoxious to abusive. On countless occasions he came close to bar fights, then backed down. He was a bulky fellow who'd taken boxing lessons as a youth, could be offensive and goad someone into anger, the laugh and walk away. All too often he went home drunk and angry. Altercations involving his family sometimes followed.

In mid-January, 1962, Wayland and Helen were back in the news:
*Cass County Sheriff's officials, aided by the FBI and the Iowa Bureau of Criminal Investigation, continue to press their search for more leads and clues in the robbery of the Wayland Hopley farm home near here Sunday night. Officers had new*

*clues Monday which indicated the three bandits had headed southwest from the farm after holding Mr. and Mrs. Hopley and Mr. and Mrs. Harold Schrauger at gunpoint for more than an hour while breaking open a safe and ransacking the house. (ANT, Jan. 16, 1962)*

The article went on to say a new pair of overshoes, believed worn by one of the armed robbers, was found near the junction of Highways 6 and 48. Then, about two miles west of Griswold on Highway 92, a green piece of cloth was found, an article that matched in size and color a mask used by one of the bandits.

The masked men arrived Sunday evening while the Hopleys and Schraugers were midway through a lengthy game of canasta. They apparently pulled into the drive without being noticed. Hearing a knock at the door, Wayland lay down his cards and responded. He backed into the house with his hands in the air and a revolver at his chest. Helen was tied to a chair; the others held at gunpoint by one while his partners in crime battered open the safe and went through pretty much every dresser and drawer in the house. They obtained a few hundred dollars in cash, including a $100 bill from Mrs. Schrauger, and three diamond rings belonging to Helen. Forced to lie face down with a gun at their back, the men were relieved of their wallets.

Investigation drug out for months. There were those who had a long-standing mistrust of anyone named Hopley, but little knowledge of the case, who came to suspect the whole thing was staged for the insurance. Then-deputy sheriff Voggesser, who was a part of the investigation, says that's absurd. He was never a Hopley cheerleader, but knows the robbery did take place. After a prolonged investigation a man named McCreary, Voggesser said, was arrested, stood trial, but was found not guilty. Voggesser believes McCleary was one of the men who committed armed robbery in the Hopley farm home. A jury simply felt there was not enough evidence.

The matter brought to mind the armed robbery years earlier in Oklahoma. Wayland's older brother was in a home invaded by gun-wielding bandits and relived of cash and jewelry. Harry's case, though, had a better outcome.

Hickory spent his time in the late 50s and early 60s with business ventures that were more costly to his parents than the robbery. He and his family still lived on Hopley land, in his father's house, but their joint farming ventures dwindled and ceased.

Rodeo misadventures included accidents. In late May of 1963, Hopley loaded a truck with rodeo stock and headed for a show in eastern Iowa. Near Massena on highway 92, in a truck he habitually drove too fast (the News Telegraph contains numerous reports of speeding tickets) he tried to pass an eastbound car driven by John Voss of Atlantic. Hopley did so as Voss was making a left turn. Hopley's 59 International clipped Voss's car, then went down an embankment. Both vehicles were extensively damaged. Some of the rodeo stock was injured.

Another problem arose on a trip to South America. Trucking animals to rodeos in Minnesota, Illinois, Missouri and a few western states was one thing. Hickory, probably with the thought of an extended get-away with his mistress in mind, decided to put on a series of rodeos in Brazil and adjoining countries. Getting there by truck was not an option. Hopley leased a cargo plane, plus pilot and co-pilot.

Old Peter, who had crossed the Atlantic on sailing ships with cargos of blooded stallions, then transported them 1,000 miles more by train, would have been interested. Peter went to great expense to minimize the possibility of injury. Hickory should have done likewise, although apparently the plane sustained more damage than the livestock. The story goes that a bronco (another account has the animal as being a bull) broke loose during the flight and kicked a hole in the side of the fuselage. This caused a few anxious moments, but the plane landed safely.

The rodeo circuit, with performances scheduled in several South American countries, ran its course. While the rodeo seems to have not been a financial success, Hickory made the trip with a young lady named Betty Short. They lingered for a while. When it came time to return to Iowa, he left the still unrepaired plane in Managua, Nicaragua, and as a result was named in yet another lawsuit.

*Wayland Hopley, Jr., of Atlantic, is named defendant in a damage action brought by Aero Enterprises, Inc., of La Port, Indiana, in the U.S. District Court in Council Bluffs.*

*The Indiana company asks $18,545 from the Atlantic man for an airplane which it leased to him for a three month period on October 17, 1963. The company states that it was advised Mr. Hopley left the damaged plane in Managua, Nicaragua, and it was necessary to send a pilot and co-pilot to return the plane to this country and restore its condition. (ANT, June 17, 1964)*

Hickory made the trip to South America with several people he employed to tend livestock and handle various responsibilities associated with putting on a rodeo. All flew down on the plane. The understanding was they'd return the same way. When the rodeo was over, Hickory walked away. The plane was abandoned, his employees left to find their own way home. When he returned his wife, who was well aware of Betty Short, was not happy. This item appeared in the Telegraph on Sept. 1, 1964:

*Shirley Hopley of Atlantic asks for a divorce from Wayland Hopley, Jr., Atlantic cattle feeder and rodeo operator, in an action filed in district court here. She asks custody of five children, $100 monthly for the support of each child, and other awards deemed necessary by the courts. She also asks for a court order to prevent Hopley from molesting her.*

*According to the petition, the couple was married here June 17, 1944, and lived together until August 15.*

The actual petition was more graphic. It alleged *"such cruel and inhuman treatment toward the plaintiff as to endanger her life and health,"* and that Hickory had *"struck her, lived openly with other women during the time of marriage, both in the U.S. and outside the continental limits."*

The petition requested that Shirley be protected from her husband by a writ of injunction barring him from molesting or interfering as she went to and from her residence.

Frank takes issue with this, saying his father was neither violent nor abusive. His mother, 91 and in poor health as this is written in 2014, has told him likewise; that regardless of what the petition claims, Hickory did not strike her or physically endanger her health.

Frank knew all about Betty Short, but doubts his father was the womanizer his reputation claimed. (The reputation, as related by those who knew him, include stories of a bear-skin rug he kept in his pickup. He allegedly boasted about the purpose, and his conquests. At his truck stop were sleeping rooms and showers for truckers. He told friends he had a room set aside for his own use. The stories of Hickory's affairs, probably exaggerated, go on and on.)

Frank feels the marriage fell apart for other reasons. As he sees it, Hickory had his problems; his wife had hers. Shirley was a hoarder, utterly disorganized. Frank said she was the type who would drive from the farm to town in the morning for a loaf of bread, then return that afternoon for a gallon of milk. His mother created dirty dishes, letting them pile up until no clean ones were left.

Frank describes his father as being a hard worker and good with livestock. He never meshed with Wayland, though, in the operation of Hopley Farms. He was treated like a hired man. He expected more. Whether the fault was with him or his father, Hickory's frustration grew. He tried other women and other ways to make himself relevant. Regardless of the reasons why they did what they did, his behavior and that of his wife had a role in the loss of the holdings began and conveyed by Peter and Edna Hopley.

Although the children of Wayland Jr., those we spoke to, did not see Hickory as being a heavy drinker, Pete's had no illusions about their father. He had a drinking problem, probably since he was a teen-ager, and it never went away. Just prior to his death he was living in Colorado. He had terminal brain cancer. On the last day of his life, one that was wintry and icy, he left his home, slipped and took a bad fall. It had not been a good day to go out. He did so as he wanted to go to a club and have a few drinks. Young Pete says there is no doubt the fall—brought on by an urge to drink—hastened his father's death.

Even as a youth, Pete, when drinking, became volatile. He was inclined to cruelty. Kendall Warne, who went to high school with Pete, remembers a beer party in what was called the "Hopley timber." Apparently Wayland and Helen were away. High school boys with beer gathered on a hilly portion of the farm, a fenced-in pasture of bluegrass shaded by groves of oak and hickory. At some point during the party

Pete wanted to go to the house. He was driving a nearly-new pick-up (probably Wayland's). Kendall went with him. Pete, driving faster than he should have, careening through the trees, spotted a hog. The animal was one of many that had been turned in to range and eat acorns. When Pete spotted the pig he swerved, then accelerated. Kendall Warne realized he was trying to run over the animal, and after a couple of tries succeeded. Warne remembers yet the squeal of the pig, the thumping sound made as the pickup passed over it, and the laughter of Pete Hopley.

That he would intentionally run down a hog, kill or maim it, then laugh, was an act that Kendall Warne has not forgotten, even though it happened well over half a century ago.

Young Pete remembers a father who was good to his family when sober. When drunk he was a different person. He had scenes with his wife. He threw a child, his daughter Pam, against a wall with such force that her head went through the sheetrock. Young Pete tells of hearing his parents fight to the extent that he and his brother Pat, both teenagers, entered the bedroom to protect their mother. At other times he could be mellow and funny. Young Pete, along with Patrick, often accompanied their father to taverns. He would drink and play cards while the boys watched, sometimes for hours. Young Pete, not old enough to do so, was there to drive his father home.

Pete was a regular at Atlantic's Elks Club, the Cardio Hotel bar, the Elbow Room, and a tavern on Walnut Street called The Office. He did not, though, ever have a reputation for womanizing.

The brothers did not get along. They seem to have not been treated equally. There may have been jealousy. Frank remembers his father's anger over the way Pete misused equipment, saying that on at least one occasion an altercation could have gotten physical had not Wayland intervened.

Pete did other things that alienated his brother's family. Shortly after Wayland's death Frank, then a teen-ager, saw a way to make a little money raising sheep. For the purpose he had his eye on a couple of acres of fenced-in pasture that hadn't been used for years. He asked Helen. She said she saw no problem and would tell Pete, who was then managing the place. Pete said no; he planned to use it himself. Frank kept watch on the bit of pasture for months. Pete never used it.

As husbands, neither got better with age. Hickory was eventually married four times. After Shirley he married Betty Short. They were divorced, then remarried and divorced again. His last wife, Carlita, was apparently a woman of ill temper. Frank told us she made a serious attempt to kill Hickory. She failed, and they were still married when he died in Florida in the 1980s.

After Pete and Margaret's less-than-idyllic honeymoon in Las Vegas, the newlyweds moved to Florida, taking with them two registered Black Angus heifers Wayland and Helen had given Margaret as a wedding gift.

The Florida venture involved Kent Feed Company and the development of a new breed of cattle—one that would combine the growth and marbling traits of Black Angus with the hardy, disease resistance of the Brahman . Wayland Hopley and Gage Kent, who founded the company in Indianola, had known each other for years. Together they bought a tract of pastureland in Florida. Theirs was not a new idea. The National Brangus Association had been formed a few years earlier and a good many cattle feeders felt the potential was there, but getting the right mix (eventually stabilized at 3/8 Brahman and 5/8 Angus) took time and experimentation. After less than two years in Florida, where their first daughter was born, Pete and Margaret moved to Georgia. There Pete was retained to manage a former plantation converted to a cattle operation. In 1957, following the birth of a second daughter, the family returned to Iowa. They moved into a house a short distance from the West Side place. For the next few years Pete farmed some with his father, drove a truck, tried auctioneering, and sold Harvestore feeding systems, and drank a lot of scotch.

Examples of Pete Hopley's careless indolence abounded. Young Pete says his father once bought a new Oldsmobile and drove if more than 60,000 miles without changing the oil. He neglected farm machinery the same way. Former neighbors remember a new combine left outside for months when there was plenty of indoor space, an otherwise good planter clogged with seed corn left in the hoppers from the year before, implements rusting and bearings failing for lack of grease.

There were those who remember him differently—drinking buddies and poker players enjoyed his company (at least up to a point)—but no one accused Pete Hopley of committing overwork. He was unreliable and it mattered not what he was doing or needed to do; when the urge to party struck him, he was on his way.

I met Pete during those years. I was probably fourteen or fifteen, just a year or so after my adventure in the "haunted" Hopley mansion. The Hopleys, like other area farmers, hired boys as day laborers; mostly to help put up hay.

During my school summers I worked, over a period of time, for two dozen farmers or more. More memorable than the pay was the food. Like most of the boys, I was thin as a day's wages but appreciated a good meal and could eat a mountain of whatever was on the table.

Farm wives were wonderful cooks. Mrs. Don Buboltz (she had a strange first name I'm no longer sure of; Zola, perhaps, or something like it) was especially good. She might serve main courses of pot roast and fried chicken at the same meal, accompanied by all the sides and followed by peach cobbler warm out of the oven. By late summer's third cutting of hay she'd be making use of the garden; boiling a bucket of sweet corn, fixing fresh peas, beans, sliced tomatoes and serving sweet peppers stuffed with cream cheese and black walnuts. If there'd been an eligible daughter I'd have gladly married into the family.

Francina Baker made ham loaf like no one else. Floy Hulsebus pounded out thin slices of beef, dredged them in something, fried them crisp and stacked 'em high. Mrs. Rex Bailey did raisin cream pie, apple crisp, strawberry pie, and she didn't want leftovers.

We ate well with the Kennedy family, and Kunzes and McGaffins as well. The Weppler ladies, like most others, understood that a few thousand calories at mid-day would sustain a body only so long. They came to the field in the afternoon with lunch; sandwiches, pickles, deviled eggs, iced tea and cake and pie.

At Hopleys, on the couple of days I was there, we were packed into a car and taken to Hopco's for a burger and fries. Dining in a restaurant was fun, but not very filling.

I wasn't around Pete enough to know him. The first impression though, was not good. He seemed slack-faced, expressing more of a sneer than a smile, his laugh not pleasant. He was husky, looked as if he could throw a bale over the roof, but tossing bales wasn't in his job description.

There was a day when two of us in the barn were falling behind. Heat in the loft was stifling, we were soaked with sweat and hay bales were falling off the elevator faster than we could stack them. Outside we could see Pete leaning on a fence talking, probably with his father. With me was a full time hired hand, a man whose name I've forgotten. He glanced outside, then said this: *"That's one of the problems with this God-damned f---ing place; too many God-damned chiefs and not enough f—ing Indians."*

To a youthful Boy Scout being raised in a strict, devout Methodist household, the words were as exquisite as fine poetry. My grades in English were not the best—I couldn't tell a participle from an interjection—but I knew a good sentence from a bad one. This one was delightful; an insightful opinion expressed in flowing, exciting, and perfectly descriptive words. I was so impressed that for days I repeated the sentiment at every opportunity, thereby committing it to permanent memory.

The hired man, I'm sure, knew what he was talking about.

# Chapter Twenty-Four

Weather records show that June of 1965 was, in southwest Iowa, wetter than normal. A series of thunderstorm rolled through, some of them violent, producing strong winds and locally heavy downpours. The last day of the month dawned hot and sticky. Hickory, who had been having marital issues for some time, was served with divorce papers the previous fall. He had not, Frank said, moved out, but was dividing his time between his family and Betty Short.

One account has him staying, on that final night in June, in what was called "the bunkhouse." Built by Harry, probably to house seasonal help and double as an office, the one room, one story building was used, during Wayland's ownership, as a guest house and party room; a temporary refuge for a friend or relative in need.

A couple of weeks earlier, in one of his numerous motor vehicle accidents, Hickory had broken his leg. He was wearing an ankle-to-hip cast.

Both men knew recent rains were capable of washing out plank bridges that spanned drainage ditches on the old bottom road. They did not give it a thought. The road was dry enough, Wayland had some business in Lewis and Hickory, unable to sit in the front seat, stretched out in the back.

Tom Pope, former neighbor of Hopley, former deputy sheriff and the man who followed Bob Voggesser as Cass County sheriff, said Wayland was flying low when he hit the washout. Helen later wrote a letter to one of Wayland's sisters (Minnie) saying this was not the case; that Wayland was not going fast at all. While this may have been the case, she doesn't explain how, being home at the time, she could be so certain.

The dirt road was across flat land, with the approach to the bridge on a slight upward grade. At the steering wheel Wayland, had he been driving slowly and watching closely, might have seen the washout in time to stop. Whether he was speeding or not (one version has him talking with Hickory in the back seat rather than watching the road) he didn't see the washout. The front of the car dropped, the hood and bumper plowed into an embankment. Wayland's chest was slammed into the steering column, and his son's weight was thrown against the back of the front seat.

Hickory would profess to believe his being in the back contributed to his father's fatal injuries, but the result may have been the same regardless. Steering columns on big-engine cars like Hopley's were not designed for safety. There were no air bags, no padded dash or steering wheel. The 1963 Chevrolet had seat belts, but Wayland didn't use them.

Bruised and shaken but otherwise uninjured, Hickory got a door open and, although impeded by his cast, sought help. Wayland was taken by ambulance to the Atlantic Hospital, where he remained until July 3. He was then transferred to Methodist Hospital in Omaha. Doctors at neither place could do much for him.

His sternum was crushed, ribs shattered and driven into his lungs. His heart was bruised and he suffered other internal injuries. For five days, with Helen at his side most of the time, other family members taking turns, blood seeped into his lungs and he slipped in and out of consciousness.

Wayland Hopley was 70 years old and knew he wouldn't live forever. He probably resented the manner; he was in much better health than Harry had been at a younger age, might have lived another decade or more, and was going out because of a thoughtless accident that could have happened when he was fourteen.

He must have known the end was at hand.

If he hadn't been told directly he understood that a visit by Roscoe Jones, which took place on Saturday, was more than a social call. Jones was Hopley's long-time attorney. One of Atlantic's best, he'd represented

Wayland and Helen through lawsuits and business transactions. Jones would not have taken long to get down to business. He was there to update a will. His client was in severe pain. Jones' notes indicate he posed as many questions as practical in a manner that could be answered with a nod of the head. Punctured lungs make breathing, and speaking, difficult.

Wayland signed his will with a shaking hand, Roscoe Jones witnessing. Jones departed and Hopley was transferred by ambulance to Omaha.

The next day, July 4, was the twenty-first anniversary of George's death.

Wayland Hopley, in the grey hours of a nighttime hospital room, with an IV helping prolong his life and control the pain, his breath coming in short gasps, must have thought of his life, of wars and death and the future of Hopley Farms.

He had experienced his share of death; mostly from a distance. He was too young to remember when his sister, Beulah, suffered a seizure from which she never recovered. He was but six when his grandmother Frances passed on. She'd been an invalid for years, and he scarcely knew she existed. Given her advanced age and long-term health failures, she probably didn't know him either.

While men died by the thousands during his war, his duty was mostly behind the lines—certainly at risk, but not to the extent of those in the trenches. He was in France when his mother and a sister died unexpectedly, their funerals long over when he returned home. His father was in California when he expired.

Even the two deaths that most impacted his life occurred while he was far away. George was killed in France. Wayland had visited brother Harry while he was a patient in Omaha, but was not at his bedside when he died.

Now, with his own death at hand, there was a lot to think about. The time for doing anything though, was nearly past—but not quite.

Frank believes the will originally provided for a division of the estate between Helen and the two sons. The deathbed change left everything to Helen.

The reasons, in Frank's view, included Pete's irresponsibility and drinking. Turning over a portion of the farm to him seemed foolish.

With Hickory there were both marital and financial issues. If he had ability he'd done little to show it. He and his father had never arrived at a mutually agreeable working arrangement. Hickory's fate with the estate was sealed, Frank believes, by his pending divorce. The immaculate Helen was not on good terms with the disorganized hoarder that was Shirley. There was another woman in the picture. Lawyers were involved. Passing property to Hickory under those circumstances was not promising. If Helen was not pleased with Hickory's wife, she was less so with his girl friend.

Wayland had reason to feel that neither son was a deserving heir. His wife knew their sons just as well. In the end it was decided to leave it all to Helen, perhaps with the hope that, in years ahead, one of their boys would reform and grow up.

Assets listed in the will included nearly 2,000 acres, the purebred Angus breeding herd, another 800 to 1,000 cattle on feed, 120 head of hogs and horses estimated to number between 50 to 60 (this is the amount of horses listed in the estate filing. Frank remembers being there when horses were counted and said there were 105. It seems likely numbers were downsized to reduce the tax burden).

Total assets, no doubt figured conservatively for tax purposes, were almost $1 million. Liabilities show that Hopley spread his debts around: he owed $1,294 to the Atlantic State Bank for a tractor, $1,300 to the Whitney Bank for another tractor and a corn planter, $1,471 came from a Des Moines bank on a hydraulic loader. There was also a long list of notes Wayland co-signed with Hickory for the truck stop and rodeo.

The big note was held by First National Bank in Kansas City. This $87,000 loan, listed as being for cattle and feed, was secured by a lien on Hopley farmland. (This appears to be a continuation of a series of loans from Metro Life of Kansas City. Metro Life, or MetLife as it is called today, dates to the Civil War. While it was typical for insurance companies to put their capital in the stock market, Metro Life preferred loans extended to sound businesses and farmers with collateral. Their limited exposure to the stock market was a factor in keeping Metro Life solvent during the market crash of '29 and the Great Depression. Peter borrowed from them, as did Harry and later Wayland. They often underwrote bank loans, including some from First National of Kansas City.)

Whatever Wayland's thoughts on a long Sunday night, breathing became increasingly difficult. Time of death was listed as 8 a.m. Monday. His body was returned to Roland's Funeral Home in Atlantic. On Tuesday evening, Helen, who had time to make plans, had the remains taken to the home north of Lewis. Young Pete, Wayland's grandson, remembers he and his brother (Patrick) scampering about the room where the coffin was on display. His mother remembers as well, saying she took measures to make their behavior a bit more appropriate. Also remembered by family members are two men who flew in for the funeral, landing either a charter or company airplane at the Atlantic airport. Margaret's understanding is that they were representatives of an insurance company Wayland owed money to. On top of existing loans, Wayland had borrowed heavily from Metro Life to buy the 1200 acres from Della after Harry's death. While these agents may have been there to pay their respects, they reportedly asked Helen for a few minutes alone with her and, so the story goes, discussed matters of a financial nature.

With the funeral over Helen proceeded to sell land to pay debts, including the big one to Metro Life. All of what had been Peter Hopley's accumulated acreage east of the river was sold in 1966 to Riverwood Farms (the Pellett family).

This left a few hundred acres west of the Nishnabotna, and farm management went to Pete.

The empire his grandfather built had prospered under Harry, slipped considerably but held on with Wayland. Pete oversaw a spiraling decline to a point from which there was no recovery. He neglected the farm, and his family.

In 1972 Margaret, having some money of her own from an investment, decided to buy what was known as the Kelloway house. Built by the founder of Walnut Grove feeds, on land east of the river purchased from Hopley Farms a few years before, the house was elegant and luxurious. Margaret's confidence in her husband was such that she had the house deeded in her name only.

June 27, 1975, marked the 25th anniversary of Pete and Margaret's wedding. He went out that day and didn't come home until the next.

"I didn't know," Margaret said, "if he was hurt, in a ditch somewhere, or with someone else." She must have thought of their honeymoon in Las Vegas, when he deposited her in a hotel room, went gambling, and left her to wonder for hours.

With Pete losing money Helen sold the site of what had been the Hopco Truck Stop. The remainder of Harry's land owned by Della's niece, Eleanor Liston, was sold to the Freund brothers in 1974.

Hickory continued to have his own problems. The change in Wayland's will could not have been good news. Divorce is often unpleasant. To Shirley's claims that he'd struck and physically abused and endangered her, lived openly with other women, was added another offense. He wasn't paying court-ordered child support.

Law enforcement officers in a small community tend to know the people. They knew the Hopley brothers and, for the most part, were not fond of either. Pete was a buffoon who drank much too much—with or without an underage son to do his driving. Hickory had his benders and girlfriends and, it seemed, neglected a wife and the five legitimate children he'd fathered.

When the court, in the early summer of 1966, issued a warrant for contempt there were officers more than happy to execute it. At about the same time word circulated that Hickory and Shirley's daughter, Nancy, was hospitalized. An officer I knew, not realizing the seriousness of her illness, made the joke that, since Hickory wouldn't buy groceries for his kids, she was probably suffering from malnutrition. Tasteless as the starvation remark was, it was repeated.

Hickory was held in contempt in more ways than one.

Nancy was diagnosed with an aggressive and fatal form of leukemia. The girl, just sixteen years of age, died about the time her father was placed under arrest.

As Bog Voggesser remembers the matter, Sheriff Ben McGill had the compassion to allow Hickory to attend his daughter's funeral. This was a bit of a risk on McGill's part, and would not have been good had any of several potential incidents resulted. Hickory gave his word— he would go to the funeral service at the Roland Funeral Home and accompany the procession to the cemetery near Lewis. Following graveside services he was to return immediately to the sheriff's office. Between the funeral and the Oakwood Cemetery he was seen, away from the procession, by Glen Green, then a Highway Patrolman. Green, knowing of the arrest warrant, radioed an inquiry. McGill was upset. Hopley was not where he should have been. The sheriff called for his apprehension and return to jail. By the time word got back to Green, he wasn't sure where Hopley was. Deputy Voggesser went looking and found Hickory at the cemetery.

Where Hickory went in the interim we don't know. Neither do we know why Froggy Goeken went to the service wearing a gun. People who knew Froggy say his behavior was often erratic, that he owned guns and liked to show them. He was acquainted with Hickory Hopley, and I've been told the two sometimes drank together. Frank, though, who was then eighteen, says his father and Froggy were not close.

Voggesser arrived, spotted Hickory, made a quick and quiet arrest and departure without even realizing Goeken was there.

With Nancy laid to rest, Pete and Helen (according to Voggesser) drove directly to the courthouse and called on the county sheriff. Pete was, as usual, vocal and obscene. Helen is said to have outdone him.

She felt the arrest of her son during a funeral was outrageous, and she employed profane language to express her views. Voggesser said she made a scene, shouting words he'd not have expected from Helen, demanded Hickory's immediate release. McGill listened for a few minutes, then told her to calm down. He'd done the family a favor letting Hickory out for the funeral, doing so with an understanding. He had reason to believe Hickory had violated that understanding. Regardless, if Helen and Pete didn't leave immediately he'd arrest them both. They left.

# Chapter Twenty-Five

Helen kept books but otherwise had never had a role in farm management and was not prepared to take one. For a few years she continued to live in the house Harry had built, letting Pete manage what was left. Her thoughts when she drove Highway 6, passing through hundreds of acres that had once belonged to her and Wayland, would be interesting to know.

Pete was what he'd been since boyhood; crude, slothful, lazy, irresponsible.

Some years on the farm were better than others, but few, if any, were good. Pete's heart wasn't in farming. He pursued other interests. His heart wasn't in them either. He laughed and partied as crops, at times, rotted in the fields and machinery rusted. Hickory's rodeo had failed, as had the truck stop and restaurant. More Hopley land, mostly in small parcels, slipped away. Then, in 1979, Tom Henningsen, owner of an Atlantic construction company, bought most of Section 27, which included the house. Helen moved to a condo on 22nd Street.

Brooke Tanner and family later bought much of what had been West Side Farm from Henningsen, who seems to have bought as an investment and as a building site for his new home, which was built on the hill west of Harry's West Side Farm buildings. Tanner had previously bought land once owned by Hopley Farms south of Marne (Harry and Wayland's purchase in 1928, which was sold during the Depression. Tanner did not buy directly from Hopley, doing so several years later).

Tanner, 73, grew up not far from the West Side place and knew some of the Hopley family. He remembers the fine home and barns and a carriage house, now torn down, that had been a comfortable quarters for guests during Harry and Wayland's time. His mother had known Harry and Della and, like others we interviewed, saw him as being a good farmer and manager. From her vantage point, it seemed things had slipped under Wayland.

With Pete they went quickly to hell.

While Helen must have understood what was taking place, there was only so much she could do. Giving Pete $50,000 to get out of town may have been one of them.

This was not the only $50,000 check to go Pete Hopley's way.

By the late 1970s, Margaret could take no more. During the divorce she retained her attorney, her estranged husband had his. Rumor has it she paid him $50k to let the divorce proceed uncontested. She says that's not exactly how it happened, but that she did pay him that amount in order to assure there would be no future complications.

She was aware of the other $50,000 pay-off; this one from Helen. Her assessment of this coincides with that of Frank and others—that it was given as an incentive for Pete to leave the area.

Frank doesn't know the total amount, but believes this was not all that Helen gave Pete over the years, even well after the farm had been lost.

Frank, sixteen years younger than Pete, had reasons to dislike him but even as time passed found the man fun to be around. The two drank together, had some good times. Pete drove expensive cars, lived well, laughed and partied. As Frank developed a growing construction business he kept in touch with his uncle. He's sure that even as her youngest son drank himself out of a farm and marriage, Helen continued to send him money.

He tells of a time after Pete was allegedly paid off and moved to Texas. Frank, in Texas on business, called on Pete and his second wife. Pete was showing his age and the effects of his life style. Beside him in the living room was an oversized ash tray piled so high with cigarette butts they were spilling over. Pete poured and the two had a few drinks. Frank says there was a Cadillac in the drive but the garage was filled to capacity with bags of garbage. Pete, he said, lacked the ambition to carry garbage to the curb, and as a result left his car set outside.

He laughed, he smoked, and he drank.

Helen lived for sixty-six years after marrying Wayland and moving onto land that old Peter Hopley owned. She died in 1982 at the age of 85. Her obituary tells us she was a member of the First United Methodist Church, PEO, Daughters of the American Revolution, WSCS, and the Atlantic Golf and Country Club.

Her estate, what there was left, went to Pete and Hickory (Wayland, Jr).

The end soon followed. Farm equity Helen passed along was primarily in the contract sale she had made to Henningsen. Four years after her death the contract—which conveyed all the remaining Hopley land west of the river, was paid off. Hckory and Pete, and their wives at the time, received a significant cash payment. There was no more inherited land to sell.

And so Hopley Farms ceased to be.

Peter Hopley spent over half a century building Cass County's most extensive crop and livestock operation. Harry Hopley, during his 40-year tenure, expanded it. Both seemed to grasp the fundamental tenet that if they were not moving forward they were destined to slip back. Wayland became ensnarled in excessive debt, but took the operation into a new era—beyond the Depression and ensuing war to the 1960s. He adapted, viewed himself as progressive, and gave signs of awareness that mechanization and technology had the potential to revolutionize farming. The decline began during his time. Whether he might have recovered had he lived another decade no one can say.

He died at a critical juncture; a time when the farming landscape was about to change, and change rapidly. Fewer people would farm more land. Good operations, those with aggressive, forward-thinking management that understood what was taking place and made solid decisions, would grow. Others would fail. There was no longer a place for everyone then engaged.

Peter and Edna Hopley's grandsons had imperfect parents, but were born with opportunity galore. For reasons we can never entirely know, they wasted it. Hickory's self-indulgence and lack of direction helped eliminate him from the equation. This left Pete, and it was just a matter of time.

In three generations the Hopley empire was built, sustained, and lost. The name no longer appears in a Cass County phone book.

Land that was once divided into fields of hay and pasture for Hopley cattle and horses is now uninterrupted corn. A few miles from what was Hopley land the tombstones of Tommy and George weather away near those of Peter and Edna and Nancy and family members who died before and after. The house Wayland built for Helen is occupied and well-taken care of, as is the West Side place Harry prepared for Della. A couple of outbuildings are still in use, including part of a storm-damaged barn with horse stalls equipped with bars.

And Harry Hopley's concrete fence posts, a few of them, still serve a purpose.

The End

# EPILOGUE

Several members of the Hopley family were interviewed for this work, and are quoted and credited.

The book has been harsh in placing a degree of blame for the loss of a fortune. Wealth, had things been different, might have passed on to the grandchildren of Helen and Wayland Hopley. It did not.

I offered the offspring of Hickory and Pete Hopley the opportunity to read a draft and offer their thoughts. Some replied, some did not.

From Peter William Hopley, ll, is the following:

We saw the end of an era with the Hopley Family that closed the chapter on Peter William Hopley's dreams. Unfortunately, much of his legacy was squandered by his children and grandchildren. I have seen hope that lays ahead with his great grandchildren. What I experienced growing up on his farm, and hearing family stories, it appears money given to people with ignoble ease and without the normal sweat, toil, and strenuous way of earning it had negative effects.

It truly was a beautiful farm! The 300 acre timber of the 1100 acre farm was glorious to wander through. It was enjoyed and explored with family and friends whilst hunting, camping, hayrides, bon-fire parties, mushroom and walnuts hunting, horseback riding, and snowmobiling. The Nishnabotna River which runs through the farm was thriving with catfish and woodland critters. The huge barns were truly feats of ingenuity. The upper wooden decks on the floors were massive. Dad told me of roller skating parties held in them. The elevator systems were innovative. The livestock holds and tack shop must have really been sights to see when they were kept in full glory. The blacksmith shop was such an adventure to rummage through. The carriage house was filled with history, buggies, and memories. Those collection of memories and artifacts seemed to stop Uncle George's death. I remember going through his foot locker and finding his uniforms with my brother. The family lake house at Spirit Lake was a generator of fond family memories. Walking from the river house up to Hopco to watch my dad call a rodeo was a pure delight. The livestock were all beautiful. There was excitement in the air and the rodeo brought people to the truck stop to eat and drink coffee. Alas, it all went away with Interstate 80.

I witnessed in my father a tragedy of what happens when father to son mentoring does not occur. On multiple occasions, I remember Dad saying that his father never gave him the attention that was bestowed upon George. Dad was sent off to multiple Military Schools as it seemed my Grandparents hadn't the time or patience with him. Dad said the family seemed too spiraled out of control when George died. He always considered himself a disappointment to his parents. However, when the others left, he and his father were the ones that stayed on the farm when the others left. I read stories that GGP Peter wrote saying all would be managed properly by Harry, yet GP Wayland was actually the one who stayed on the farm. As I believe Harry was GGP's oldest boy, so was George to GP Wayland. Dad always said it was the English way…

It seems Dad never found his niche or true happiness in life. After the farm was sold in 1975, he began drinking even more heavily. When I did interact with him it was mostly when he was under the influence. We did have fun times snowmobiling, boating, visiting other families, but no bonding through working hard together. I think he never had any real tangible skills other that auctioneering, truck driving. His marriage eroded ending in a divorced in 1979.

I am grateful for the self-discovery that occurred will growing up on the farm. I believe it forced a function of ingenuity, simplicity, and humility that have served me well my whole life.

I thank God for my Mother and her patience and support with me. She had a hard time with me. I ended up quitting school in the 10th grade, however, I received my GED the same year. She never gave up. She drove me to work to the beef plant in Oakland, and later to my construction jobs. She sprang me out of jail for petty theft and driving infractions. She was also smart enough to let me stay in jail a couple weekends to get a taste of what could come if I didn't straighten out. After working a construction job in Texas I decided to go back to school. I followed my girlfriend who was doing the same. Mom gladly helped me out with finances in order to attend DMACC.

After two years of college I found myself less focused on its value, and my grades began falling. I met a USMC recruiter in the local gym and set up an appointment to see him.

I believe I later learned the value of money through the school of hard knocks.

I joined the USMC as an enlisted man with a contract for air traffic control but was assigned to aviation support. I married and had two beautiful girls (Chelsea and Mackenzie).

After my first overseas unaccompanied tour, I divorced. Two years after that divorce I re-married, and remain so after 20 years. We have a beautiful daughter Alexandria. Chelsea has recently blessed us with a grandson named Dyami.

After many military occupational specialties schools (over eighteen years in mechanical, electrical, avionics, ordnance, aviation support equipment, facilities operations, security management, logistics management, Water Safety Survival Instructor, USCG 50 ton Captains license, combat aircrew .50 cal gunner, and leadership) I was then selected and promoted to Warrant Officer. I went thought The Basic Officers School at Quantico at the age of 40. I was assigned as a squadron Maintenance/Avionics/Ordnance/Logistics Officer. Apparently the discipline I was lacking was provided by the USMC.

As soon as I was promoted as an officer, I was sent off to combat operations in Kuwait for Operation Southern Watch and Operation Enduring Freedom. Then later to Iraq for Operation Iraqi Freedom for two separate tours. While in Iraq I received my Bachelor's degree. Those combat tours and training deployments lasted a decade. I retired in 2010, in Hawaii after nearly 28 years' service.

Throughout my career, my mother and her husband came and visited me while stationed domestically and abroad to several countries

(Tennessee, South Carolina, Florida, Hawaii, Japan, and Guatemala). I visited my Dad on several occasions in Missouri, Texas, and Colorado, and stayed in phone contact with him until he died in 2000.

I started my own company in 2009 before retiring. It was formed to provide offshore ocean training and target practice for the DOD and visiting foreign military. The company also provides offshore ocean escort boat support for watersports races and events. It also provides surfacing attenuation testing for the Hawaii Department of Education and Parks and Recreation for playgrounds. Additionally the company does construction in Hawaii, and snow and ice removal for the Veterans Administration in the Midwest.

In addition to running my company, I recently took a job at the Hale Koa Hotel in downtown Waikiki as the Assistant Chief Engineer.

We live on the island of Oahu in a beautiful condo on the water. Our view overlooks our boat, and Diamond Head. Additionally, there are spectacular views of lush mountain ranges, sunrises, and sunsets. By the grace of God, and hard work, I am truly blessed.

Peter William Hopley, ll

--------------

Pamela Hopley Dorris writes that she married Wayne Dorris after graduating from Atlantic High School. He enlisted in the Air Force and they served for twenty-four years. They have three sons, all of which are now in the military. Pamela and Wayne live in Universal City, Texas, and work for the school district.

--------------

From Frank Hopley:
"I would like to thank Roy Marshall for his detailed work into my family going back 150 years. His way of weaving story with history resulted in an interesting read. After graduating from high school in 1966, I left a very difficult era in my life. During my school years my parents were going through a divorce. My grandfather died, my sister

died, my dad was put in jail, the house in which I was born and raised was sold, and my mom and sisters moved to California. All the poor decisions that were made and all personal problems that were not dealt with properly came to a head. So I look at that part of my life with a lot of negative thoughts. Benefitting from my dad teaching me good work ethics, I was able to move on.

I had not given this era or my family much thought until Roy Marshall called. Reading his manuscript gave me a more balanced view of my family history, learning things about my ancestors which I would have never known. I suppose I could sum it up with the old saying: "Life is too short to make all the mistakes yourself—learn from the mistakes of others."

And to quote King Solomon, "There is nothing new under the sun." My family's story is not unique in that one generation creates extreme wealth, the second generation maintains it, the third generation goes through it like a big stud horse through clover, and the fourth generation starts all over at the bottom again, and in my case on the end of a scoop shovel working construction on I80.

Through the grace of God I have been able to overcome much of the baggage handed me from my family of origin, although I am still in the process. While I have not even come close to the financial success of my great-grandfather, Peter, I have managed to get to a place of comfort and peace, which for me is a successful life."

Wayland Arrowsmith Hopley lll    (January 19, 2015)

www.ingramcontent.com/pod-product-compliance
Lightning Source LLC
Chambersburg PA
CBHW051952090426
42741CB00008B/1357

9 7 8 1 5 9 3 3 0 8 7 6 6